Pine Tree Quilts

Perfect Patchwork Piecing

Pine Tree Quilts

Perfect Patchwork Piecing

Lois Embree Arnold

American Quilter's Society

P. O. Box 3290 • Paducah, KY 42002-3290

e-mail: info@AQSquilt.com

Located in Paducah, Kentucky, the American Quilter's Society (AQS) is dedicated to promoting the accomplishments of today's quilters. Through its publications and events, AQS strives to honor today's quiltmakers and their work and to inspire future creativity and innovation in quiltmaking.

Editor: BARBARA SMITH
Graphic Design: LISA M. CLARK
Cover Design: MICHAEL BUCKINGHAM
Photography: CHARLES R. LYNCH

Library of Congress Cataloging-in-Publication Data

Arnold, Lois Embree.
    Pine tree quilts : perfect patchwork piecing / by Lois Embree Arnold.
        p. cm.
    1. Patchwork--Patterns. 2. Quilting--Patterns. 3. Pine tree in art.
I. Title.
TT835 .A76 2000
746.46'041--dc21
                                    00-012525
ISBN 1-57432-749-6

Additional copies of this book may be ordered from the American Quilter's Society, PO Box 3290, Paducah, KY 42002-3290, or online at: info@AQSquilt.com.

This book is dedicated to the memory of my mother, Dora McGee Embree. Her quilts were freely given to family, friends, and those in need. She tirelessly hand pieced and hand quilted in the evenings after a hard day of work on the farm. She passed the love of quilting on to others and generously gave her time to show them how to quilt.

I can't remember ever sleeping without a quilt on my bed. Her quilts warmed my body, but it was her love and generosity that warmed my heart. Thank you, Mom.

Acknowledgments

Nothing in life is accomplished alone. Without the help and support of a great many people, this book would never have been started, much less finished. Thank you to the members of the Nimble Thimbles Chapter of the Arizona Quilter's Guild, to the many friends who made quilts especially for use in this book, to those who allowed their quilts to be photographed, and to those who gave me names of people who own antique pine tree quilts that might be used in the book or for my education. Thank you, also to the makers of the Electric Quilt™ program, which was used in designing many of the projects for the book and many that didn't make it into the book, but will be made eventually.

Special thanks go to my small group, the Therapy Group Quilters, Linda Braun, Joyce Buchberger, Maggie Keller, Diane Pitchford, and Linda Yantis, who put up with my incessant talk about the many things yet to be done and loved me anyway. To Lorinda Lie who supported me via e-mail with encouraging words and good advice, I give a heartfelt, thank you. I owe many "thank yous" to Lynn Kough, who asked just the right questions and reminded me of details known only to those who have written their own books. An enormous "thank you" goes to Bonnie Browning who suggested that I should write a book in the first place and who has encouraged me every step of the way.

Most of all, I'd like to thank my children, Mindy, Beth, and Jeff, who believed in me. I especially want to thank my dear husband, Gary, who I'm sure whispered these words in my ear even when I was asleep, "Focus, Lois, Focus!"

To all of these people and the many from whom I've learned so much over the years in classes and to the manufacturers of all the wonderful products and fabrics available to quilters today, "thank you," from the bottom of my heart!

Contents

Introduction

When we hear the words "pine trees," our minds may picture a peaceful cabin in the woods, cozy nights by the fireplace, and cool breezes under the shade of one of these majestic trees. We, as quilters, also picture Pine Tree blocks and quilts. The block most often referred to as the Pine Tree is not just one, but a group of very similar blocks. However similar, they are as diverse as the varieties of evergreens they represent, and the quilts are as individual as the quiltmakers.

There are a few other blocks called Pine Tree that are based on an isosceles triangle (a triangle with two legs longer than the base is wide). This is the shape we imagine when we think of a Christmas tree. This group includes simple paper-pieced blocks as well as more complex pieced blocks. Other Pine Trees are made in a diamond shape, and some have curved piecing or appliqué.

In Chapter One, you will find examples of the various blocks and learn the other names these blocks are sometimes called. Because a pine tree would not be complete without its pine cones, you will also find Pine Cone and Pine Burr blocks. A short history of the pine tree and its significance to the early settlers is provided in Chapter Two.

The piecing techniques illustrated in Chapter Three will help you make half-square triangle units quickly, easily, and accurately. The use of templates with precision hand and machine piecing, plus a method for combining templates with quick piecing techniques, are also included. You will learn tricks for stitching the block rows so that the triangle tips will appear crisp, clean, and sharp, reminiscent of the pine needles they represent. Appliqué and paper-piecing techniques are illustrated in the chapter as well as tips for finishing a quilt and drafting new sizes of Pine Tree blocks to suit your needs.

The patterns in Chapter Four have been tested for accuracy to ensure your success. Templates are included for your convenience. Pine Tree quilt plans in the project section contain fabric requirements and detailed directions enabling you to begin stitching your Pine Tree quilt almost immediately. Do remember with fabric, more variety is better! A number of the quilts are made with many different fabrics, giving a scrap look. Some of the patches appear to be made from the same fabric until examined more closely.

A gallery of modern and antique quilts may inspire you to stitch your own forest, so you can dream of being perpetually on vacation in a lovely mountain cabin under the pines. Enjoy!

Chapter 1

Pine Tree Family

You might assume there is a single block called "Pine Tree," but in reality, there are a variety of blocks that bear the name. Pine Tree blocks have in common rows of triangles representing branches, and each block has a trunk unit. The blocks are drawn on grids ranging from five to 16 units.

The trunk units vary as well. Many of them contain a rectangle with a large half-square triangle at the top to form the base of the branches and another half-square triangle at the bottom to indicate the ground. There are also Pine Tree blocks that have curved trunks appliquéd to the background in place of pieced rectangular trunks.

In most blocks, the branches are in rows made of half-square triangles (Blocks 1–30 and 32–36). In a few blocks, the branch rows are formed by squares (Block 31). Some branches are divided into cone-shaped pieces (Block 37) or made of diamonds (Block 38).

In addition to the traditional Pine Tree, there are blocks sewn Log Cabin fashion with rectangular branches (Block 39) or with angled branch ends topped with triangles (Block 40).

In another block, called "Trail of the Lonesome Pine," curved triangles are used as branches (Block 41).

Other blocks resemble flying geese units (Blocks 42 and 43). These are often foundation pieced. Other trees are made from Christmas-tree-shaped triangles (Block 44).

There are related blocks called "Pine Cone" and "Pine Burr." They represent the cones on the trees and vary from simple star shapes to more complicated feathered-star blocks.

Five Grid

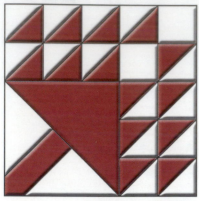

Block 1

Block 2

Block 3

Six Grid

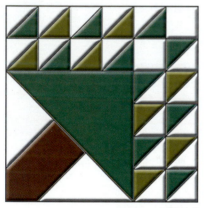

Block 4

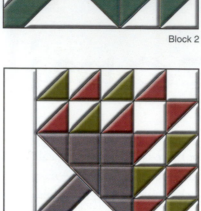

Block 5

Block 6

Seven Grid

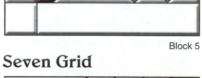

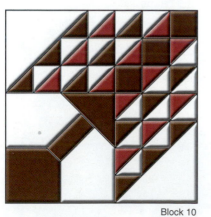

Block 7

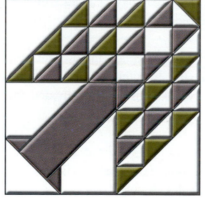

Block 8

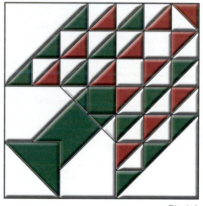

Block 9

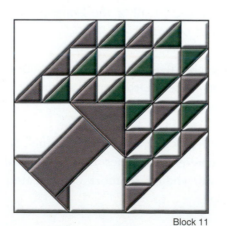

Block 10

Block 11

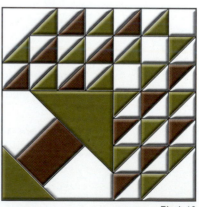

Block 12

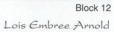

Eight Grid

Block 13

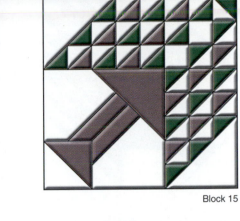

Block 14

Block 15

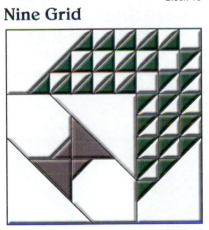

Block 16

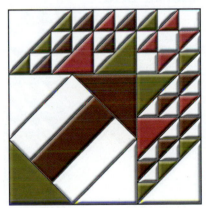

Block 17

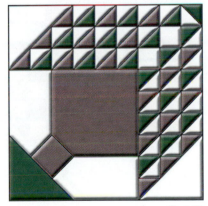

Block 18

Nine Grid

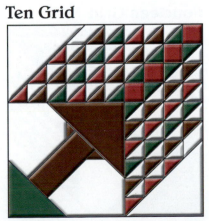

Block 19

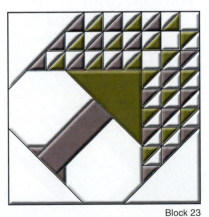

Block 20

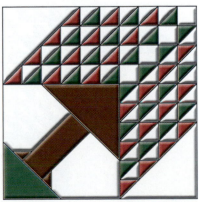

Block 21

Ten Grid

Block 22

Block 23

Block 24

Ten Grid continued

Block 25

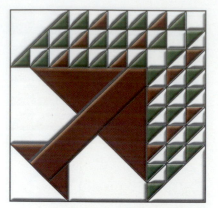

Block 26

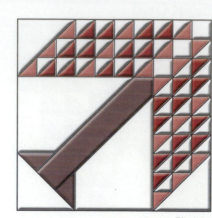

Block 27

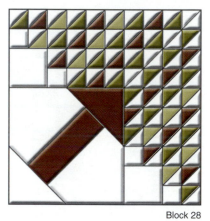

Block 28

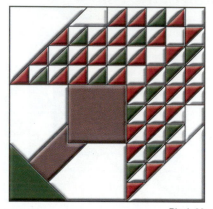

Block 29

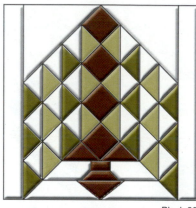

Block 30

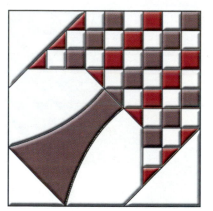

Block 31

Eleven Grid

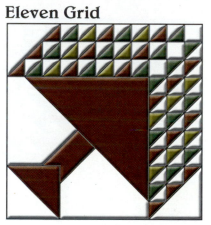

Block 32

Twelve Grid

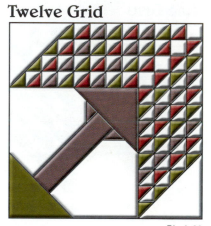

Block 33

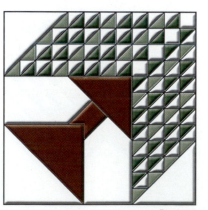

Block 34

Thirteen Grid

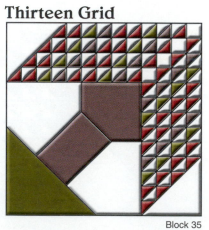

Block 35

Fourteen Grid

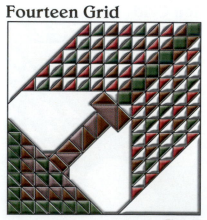

Block 36

Cones

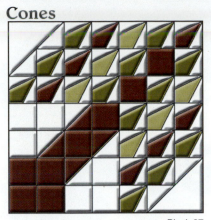

Block 37

Diamonds

Block 38

Log Cabins

Block 39

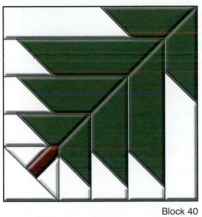

Block 40

Trail of the Lonesome Pine

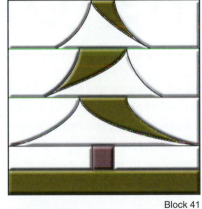

Block 41

Flying Geese

Block 42

Block 43

Christmas Tree

Block 44

Pine Burrs

Block 45

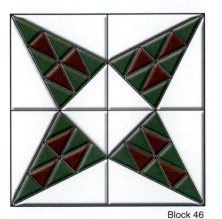

Block 46

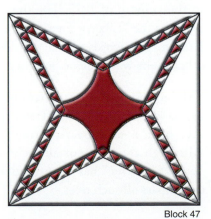

Block 47

Block 48

Chapter 2

Pine Tree History

Pine trees have played an important role in American history. The first explorers to set foot on what is now American soil came looking not for trees, but for treasure. Finding little, the men convinced their sponsors they had found "treasure" in the trees. Because wood was scarce in England, these entrepreneurs were able to provide wood for building ships, and the tall pines were perfect for their needs.

When the early settlers began to arrive, the trees again became treasure as they provided both the raw material to build homes and the fuel to warm those homes. Pine trees also provided humble furnishings to replace those left behind. If the homes were not already in a wooded area, the trees were planted in rows surrounding the houses to provide protection against hostile winds.

Pine trees truly became a treasure when the pine tree shilling was minted in Massachusetts in 1652. This shilling remained in circulation through 1682.

Photo 2–1
Copy of
pine tree shilling,
minted 1652 to 1682.

The first naval flag to fly over American ships bore the pine tree symbol. The Pine Tree Flag is a generic name for a variety of flags used both by Massachusetts and by New England from 1686 to 1776. A Pine Tree Flag with these words "Appeal to Heaven" was used as George Washington led his men in the autumn of 1775. The tree in the middle of this flag is reported to depict the "Liberty Tree" where the Sons of Liberty would meet in Boston. The words reflect the deep belief the revolutionaries shared that theirs was a divine purpose.

The states of Maine and Vermont still have pine trees on their state flags. Maine is known as the Pine Tree State, and 19 of the 50 states have needle-bearing trees as their state trees. Although they are not all technically pine trees, the term "pine tree" has been used as a generic term to encompass all such trees.

With this history, the pine tree has long been a symbol of faith, loyalty, steadfastness, and eternal life. Is it any wonder, then, that this became a popular motif in quilts? Pine Tree quilts in one variation or another are displayed in nearly every quilt show.

The earliest documented Tree of Life quilts are elaborate broderie perse versions. They were patterned after the *palampore*, a word derived from the Persian and Hindi languages, meaning bedcover.

This is the form of the pine tree that was made in the first half of the 1800s and may have been what Dolores Hinson in her *Quilting Manual* referred to when she said, "Trees have been very popular since the earliest Colonial days." Ruth Finley in her book, *Old Patchwork Quilts*, also referred to the Pine Tree quilts as dating from the colonial days and wrote that they were made in all 13 colonies. While this has not been documented, one cannot deny the significance of the pine tree in colonial America.

The Pine Tree quilt pieced of triangles became popular in the latter half of the 1800s. Many examples of this type have survived and have been documented by experts in dating quilts. One example in the book *New York Beauties, Quilts from the Empire State* is dated 1860 or later. Many of these quilts came to light in the state documentation days that have been held by quilt groups in nearly every state of the Union.

The traditional versions were primarily two-color quilts. Green and white, red and white, and blue and white were the most common colors used (Photo 2–2). Some of the greens were fugitive and appear as tan in the quilts that have survived (Photo 2–3). Some of the quilts with red and green in the branches have also changed color through the years, fading to a soft tan and almost orange (Photos 2–4 and 2–6.) Other versions feature brown trunks with predominately green triangles representing the branches. A few red triangles among the green ones in a quilt represent fruit (Photo 2–5). Charming examples of quilts made from scraps are also found (Photo 2–7).

Photo 2–2
Pine Tree quilt, 1890–1910, 63" x 80". Example of a red and white quilt. Courtesy of Xenia Cord, Legacy Quilts.

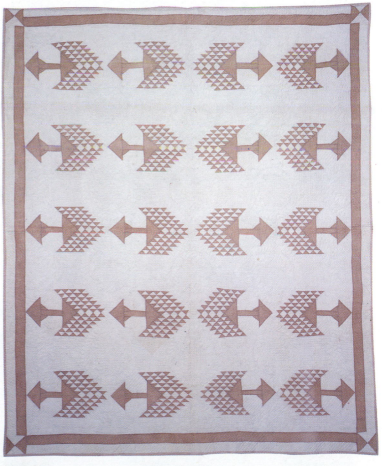

Photo 2–3
Pine Tree quilt, c. 1880, 74" x 87". Example of fugitive green. Collection of the author.

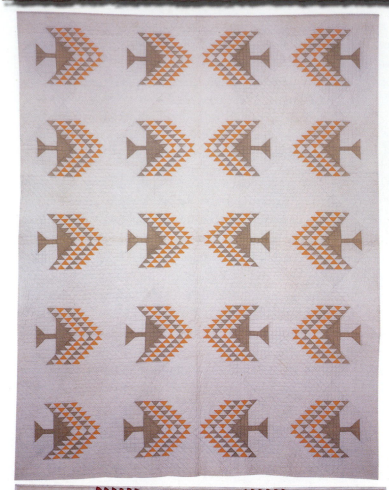

Detail of Pine Tree quilt.

Photo 2–4
Pine Tree quilt (with detail at right), c. 1900, 68" x 86". This example exhibiting fugitive red was made for Cora Yardly by her Great-aunt Cora. Collection of Dorothy Imig.

Photo 2–5
Quilt top, 1880–1900, 66" x 78". Red triangles represent fruit. Collection of the author.

Photo 2–6
Pine Tree quilt, c. 1850, 71" x 73". Example of fugitive red. Collection of Rosie Grinstead.

Photo 2–7
Scrap quilt, c. 1930, 65" x 88". Collection of the author.

and New Testaments of the Bible. Although the tree referred to in the Garden of Eden was a fruit-bearing tree, the quilter simply used the pine tree and added a few red triangles to represent the fruit.

Other names that this familiar block has carried are Norway Pine, Proud Pine, Maine's Spreading Pine, and Christmas Tree. Quilters even used the same pattern, but gave it the name of other trees, such as Apple Tree and Patch Blossom. Other quilters substituted squares (Photo 2–8) or diamonds for the triangles representing the branches and called the block Cherry Tree, Little Beech Tree, Lozenge, or Live Oak. Another variation, called the Cone Tree, contains isosceles triangles.

The pattern evolved into tall and narrow as well as short and squatty blocks. Some variations contained as few as two rows of triangles to represent the branches and some as many as seven. The use of three rows is the version most often seen in this group of patterns. Some variations expose the "roots" beneath the trunk by using triangles to represent them. The trunk is pieced, appliquéd, or divided into squares and triangles, depending on the origin of the pattern and the name by which it is called. Some variations have rows or branches that are equal, while others have uneven rows. In some versions, a solid trunk runs through the branches. In some variations, a top triangle is added to give more definition to the tip of the tree.

Marguerite Ickis in *The Standard Book of Quiltmaking and Collecting* gives these instructions for constructing the Pine Tree block, "After the triangles in the tree are pieced together, turn in all outside edges as the tree must be appliquéd to the block. Place it on the block (the center crease will guide you), baste to the background and add trunk to the lower half. Appliqué with small hemming stitches."

It is an interesting method for stitching this block. Perhaps this was a way to avoid piecing the odd shapes often found in the trunk area.

The Pine Tree block was printed in 1894 in the *Ohio Farmer* under the name Temperance Tree. The block, however, has no documented ties to the Woman's Christian Temperance Union. Carrie Hall and Rose Kretsinger also referred to the Pine Tree as the Temperance Tree in their book, *Romance of the Patchwork Quilt in America*. There is at least one Pine Tree quilt that has a reference to temperance in the embroidery, so undocumented or not, the name was used by women to state their opinion. The name lost favor along with the repeal of Prohibition in 1933. The Pine Tree was the first block to appear in the famed *Kansas City Star* series. The issue is dated September 22, 1928.

The Pine Tree block has enjoyed many names, some connected with political causes, as in the case of the Temperance Tree, and many with religious associations. Names like Tree of Paradise, Tree of Life, and Tree of Temptation referred to trees in both the Old

Most of the quilts dating from the late nineteenth and early twentieth centuries kept the look of separate pine trees. Most of these quilters set the Pine Tree on point, facing either the top of the quilt or the center. Some quilters kept the blocks set square, resulting in

Photo 2–8
Pine Tree quilt, 69" x 89". Sometimes squares were substituted for triangles. Collection of the author.

trees that appear to bend in the wind (Photo 2–9). Though a few quiltmakers experimented with the design to achieve patterns that nearly make the pine tree disappear into the setting, most quilters, even today, usually keep the integrity of the tree intact.

Strip-piecing is another simple way to achieve a Pine Tree look. These trees date to the *Old Chelsea Station* patterns. The author combined both paper piecing and strip piecing for a block used in a group exchange (Photo 2–10).

In the late 1980s, paper piecing became a popular method of constructing Pine Trees. These are often simple isosceles triangles with a trunk unit (Photo 2–11) that are reminiscent of the traditional Tall Pine pattern. These trees can be easily subdivided to make use of a variety of scrap fabrics. Because of their small size, blocks of this type are often found in Christmas wall quilts and are sometimes combined with simple "cabin" shapes.

Simple tree shapes, outlined with a buttonhole appliqué technique, have also become popular. Many of the recent "Northwoods" quilts sport these whimsical, folk-art trees The quilt in Photo 2–12 is an example of tree blocks that were first pieced and then appliquéd in this manner on the background squares. In this quilt, the trees are cheerful and bright, containing a variety of 1940s prints. The buttonhole stitch is sewn upside down, adding to the folk-art look.

Whether you choose one of the many traditional Pine Tree patterns or a contemporary paper-pieced version, you will join a host of other quilters who, for generations, have paid homage to the humble pine.

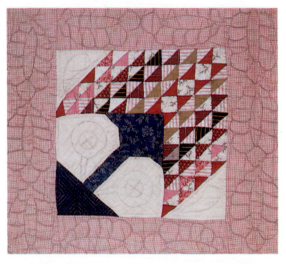

Detail of Pine Tree quilt.

Photo 2–9
Pine Tree quilt (with detail above), c. 1875, 70" x 78". Blocks were sometimes set square. Collection of the author.

Photo 2–10
Pine Tree block, 12" x 12". Paper-pieced by the author.

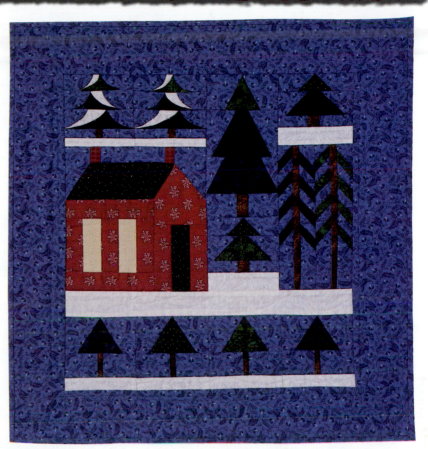

Photo 2–11
Pine Tree sampler, 1998, 24" x 25". Made by the author.
Collection of Linda Braun. (Pattern begins on page 46.)

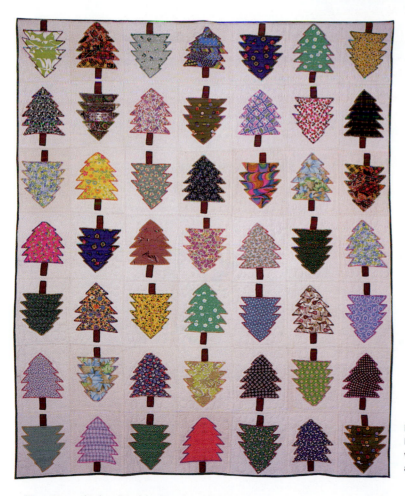

Detail of Northwoods quilt.

Photo 2–12
Northwoods quilt (with detail at right), c. 1945, 70" x 85". Folk-art trees were first pieced and then appliquéd to the background. Collection of the author. (Pattern for contemporary adaptation begins on page 73.)

A Walk in the Pine Forest

Since the very first Pine Tree quilt was made, the patterns associated with the name have been popular with quilters. Almost every quilt show around the country will have an entry made from one of this group of patterns. Quilters everywhere seem to enjoy creating their very own versions to adorn their beds and walls. Take a walk through this pine forest of quilts.

PINE BURR (37" x 37") by Lynn G. Kough.
Without pine cones, sometimes called burrs, there would be no pine trees. Lynn machine pieced and machine quilted her quartet of pine burrs in Christmas reds and greens.

SHADOWS IN THE SNOW (85" x 104") by Carol Butzke.
The Wisconsin winters and her family's love of skiing inspired this wonderful blue and white version of the Pine Tree quilt. The border was designed by using a collection of elements from Jinny Beyer's *Quilter's Album of Blocks and Borders* book. Carol hand quilted a scene of her family cross-country skiing, in the lower border, which is only visible from the back. Machine pieced and hand quilted.

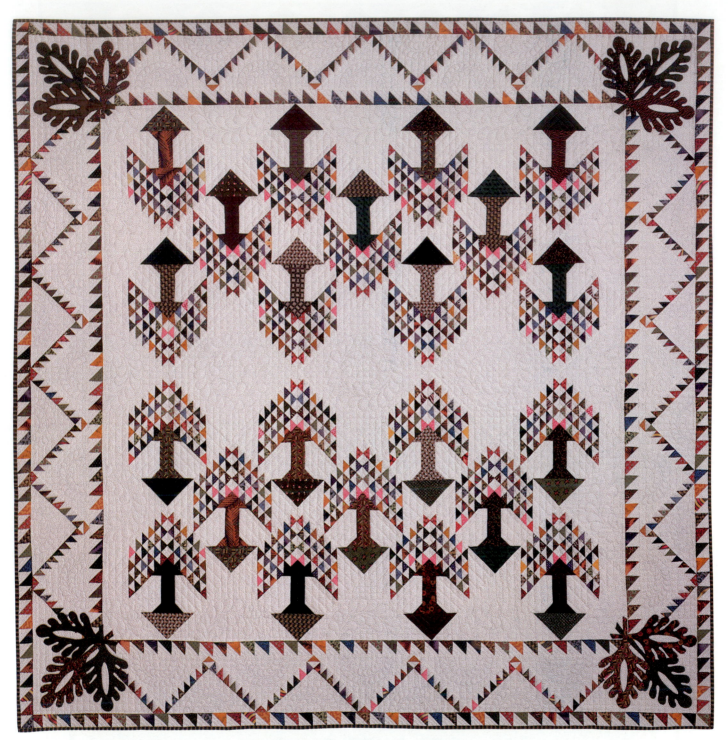

PINE TREE (72" x 72") by Gerry Sweem.
Machine pieced, hand appliquéd, and hand quilted. Inspired by a Pine Tree quilt pictured in Roderick Kiracofe's book, *The American Quilt* (Clarkson N. Potter, Inc., 1993) and by the setting of a quilt from the collection of Paul Pilgrim and Gerald Roy, Gerry created her own version, adding appliquéd leaves in the corners for impact. Photo by Melisa Karlin Mahoney, courtesy of *Quilter's Newsletter Magazine*.

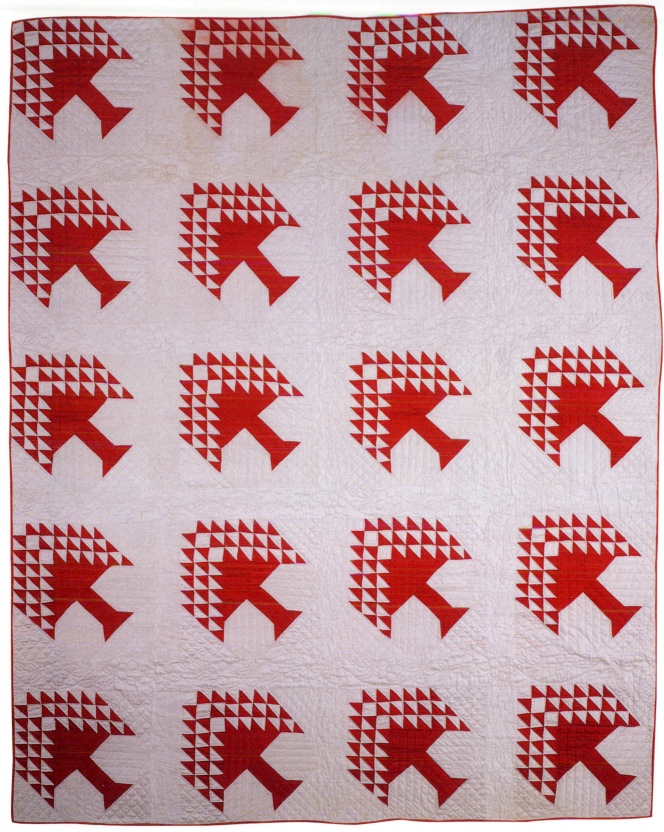

PINE TREE QUILT (75" x 93"), c. 1930, made by Mary Josephine Smith Lawler (1873–1958).
Pieced cotton sateen. Private collection, photo courtesy of Al Abrams Photography.

ANTIQUE TREE OF LIFE (76" x 84"), c. 1880–1900.
Made in Cass Co., Indiana. Courtesy of Xenia Cord, Legacy Quilts.

TALL PINES (80" x 100") designed by Carol Hannon.

Machine pieced by Carol Hannon and machine quilted by Fran Martinez. This quilt is a contemporary version of a traditional pattern made even more contemporary by paper piecing the tall pine blocks. Carol made this quilt for her son to take to college.

ONLY GOD CAN MAKE SOMETHING PERFECT (80½" x 98") designed by Heidi Vogeny.
Machine pieced by Heidi and friends, machine quilted by Louise Haley. Heidi collected Pine Tree blocks from a special-interest group
in her quilt guild and pieced the blocks together for this wonderful, traditional Pine Tree quilt.

ORANGE TREE PINE (19" x 19") by Diane Pitchford.
Diane machine pieced, hand appliquéd, and machine quilted this wall quilt for the author as a Christmas gift,
adding a note that the author should come out of the woods, occasionally. Collection of the author.

CABIN FEVER (53" x 57") by Susan Mitchell, 1999.
Machine pieced and machine quilted. After completing this Pine Tree quilt with red Irish Chain, Susan decided that the trees could have easily been paper pieced.

Chapter 3

Basic Instructions

GENERAL TOOLS AND SUPPLIES

The basic list of tools needed to piece or appliqué quilts is relatively small. The list becomes longer when optional and nice-to-have tools are included. The following items will be needed for making the projects:

Template materials
    freezer paper
    template plastic
Marking tools
Scissors
    paper
    fabric
    embroidery (optional)
Rotary cutter

Rotary mat
Acrylic rulers
Sewing machine
Needles
Thread
Pins
Iron and ironing board
Seam ripper
Stiletto

Many things can be used as template material, but **freezer paper** works well if you are making only a few blocks. Draw or trace the design on the dull side of the freezer paper and cut the freezer paper drawing apart to make templates. Press them, shiny side down, on the appropriate fabrics. It is a matter of preference whether they are ironed to the front or the back of the fabric. When pressing a template to the wrong side, remember that an asymmetrical design will produce a mirror image. If a design is to face a particular direction, use your master pattern to draw the reverse image on another sheet of freezer paper. Use the reverse image for cutting templates to press on the back of the fabric.

Template plastic makes the most durable templates. This transparent or translucent material is easy to place over the design to trace the template shape. In addition, when a clear template is used, a specific portion of the fabric design can be selected. Use a rotary cutter fitted with an old blade or a craft knife and straight edge to cut on the inside of the drawn line for the most accurate template.

Hand-piecing templates do not include seam allowances. The line drawn on the template is the sewing line. Add seam allowances to the fabric pieces by cutting ¼" outside the drawn line, by eye.

Machine-piecing templates may include seam allowances if you are using an accurate ¼" presser foot or if your sewing machine has an accurate ¼" marked on the throat plate. Templates that do not include seam allowances can be used for precision machine piecing. The line drawn on the fabric becomes the sewing line as is done in hand piecing.

Scissors should be very sharp. **Paper scissors** for cutting freezer paper, cardboard, or template material should be used only for this purpose. **Dressmaker shears** can be used to cut fabric pieces in place of a rotary cutter and should be used only on fabric to keep them sharp. Small embroidery scissors for clipping threads, whether sewing by hand or on the machine, are invaluable. **Embroidery scissors** are essential in hand appliqué for clipping precisely into corners. Clearly mark scissors "paper only" or "fabric only." You may even need to hide the fabric-only scissors from your family to keep them sharp!

Rotary cutters fitted with new blades are ideal for cutting fabric. Rotary cutters, in conjunction with special mats and rulers, have revolutionized cutting fabric pieces and strips. A second rotary cutter with an old blade is a great addition and useful for cutting paper and template materials.

There are many types of **sewing machines** on the market. A machine with a needle-down position and a knee lift are ideal, but any sewing machine will do. Sewing machines need to be maintained, oiled, and cleaned on a regular basis by following the manufacturer's guidelines. Each time the bobbin is removed from the case, brush the lint from the case and feed dogs, and oil the machine according to the guidelines usually found in the manual. The use of canned air will help remove dust and lint from these areas.

There are several types of **needles** used for quilt-making. For machine work, use the brand recommended by the manufacturer of your machine. The type of needle best suited to sewing cotton is sharp and fine. A size 80/12 quilting or jean needle works well. For paper piecing, use a 90/14 needle because it pierces the paper better, making removal easier.

For hand stitching, a long, sharp needle, called a "Sharp," is used. Sharps come in a variety of sizes. Start with a 10 and go up or down in size according to what feels comfortable for you. Needle sizes are smaller and finer the larger the number; that is, a 12 is smaller than a 10. Straw needles and milliners needles fall into this category and can be used for needle-turn appliqué.

For hand quilting, the needles used are called "Betweens." New quilters may find it helpful to buy a package of needles containing a variety of sizes. Needles vary from manufacturer to manufacturer, and it may take some experimenting to find the one that works best for you. Needles come in sizes from 7, the largest, to 12, the smallest. Not only do Betweens become finer as the number gets higher, but they also become shorter.

For machine quilting, choose the needle best suited to the type of thread used. The 80/12 quilting needle works well with cotton. For specialty threads, an embroidery needle may be needed. These have larger eyes to accommodate the thicker thread.

PIECING TECHNIQUES
Hand piecing

Use templates to transfer the block pattern shapes to the wrong side of the selected fabrics. Draw around a template with a very sharp pencil or a mechanical pencil. Cut the fabric shape ¼" outside the drawn line.

Place the two pieces to be joined right sides together, matching the ends of the drawn lines. At each end of the line, insert the point of a pin through both pieces until the pin head rests against the fabric. These are positioning pins. To secure the pieces for sewing, pin between the two positioning pins at ½" to 1" intervals, making sure the pin passes through the sewing line on both pieces (Figure 3–1.) Take a small "bite" out of the fabric to bring the point of the pin back out on the surface facing you. Pull the positioning pins out far enough to take a small "bite" in the fabric after all other pins are in place.

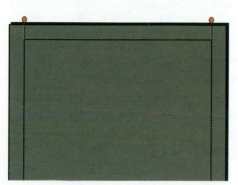

Figure 3–1.
Use positioning pins at each end of the sewing line.

Begin sewing with a backstitch ¼" from the end. Sew to the beginning of the line and backstitch. Turn and sew toward the other end, backstitching every three or four stitches. Backstitch at the end, turn and sew approximately ¼" in the other direction again, ending with a backstitch. Do not sew past the ends of the seam line so the allowances will remain free to be pressed in any direction desired. A small knot may be tied at each joining. Simply wrap the thread around the needle once, reinsert it, and bring it to the surface again.

Machine piecing

Pin the patches together every ½" to 1". Use a ¼" seam allowance, measured on the presser foot or throat plate, to sew from raw edge to raw edge. Maintaining an accurate ¼" seam allowance is critical for piecing blocks that fit together. Press seam allowances toward the darker fabric whenever possible. When it is not possible, try to press allowances so that when units of patches are sewn together, the allowances at the joined seams will lie in opposite directions (Figure 3–2).

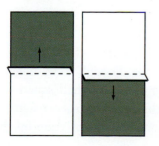

Figure 3–2.
Wherever possible, press one unit's allowances in one direction and the adjacent unit's in the opposite direction.

Precision machine piecing

In precision machine piecing, you sew on the drawn seam lines. Pin the pieces as you would for hand piecing. Begin sewing ¼" away from the beginning end of the seam line and sew toward that end. Lift the presser foot and turn the fabric 180 degrees. Sew back along the sewing line to the opposite end. Lift the presser foot again, turn the fabric 180 degrees, and take a few stitches to end the stitching line (Figure 3–3). These 180-degree turns take the place of backstitching at the beginning and end of a line. As with hand sewing, the seam allowances are free and can be pressed in any direction desired.

Figure 3–3.
Begin ¼" from one end of stitching line. Sew to the end of the line, rotate 180˚. Sew to opposite end, rotate 180˚, and stitch a few stitches to replace backstitching at each end.

Hand and machine combined

Combining hand and machine piecing makes projects portable. Use the machine to sew a number of like units, then hand sew the units together while you are traveling, or anywhere hand piecing can be done.

Half-squares make excellent carry-along units. A half-square is made from two 90-degree triangles sewn together, creating a square with a diagonal seam. They are usually made with a light and a dark fabric for contrast. Sew a bunch of half-squares on the sewing machine. Make a plastic template the finished size of the half-square unit and use the template to draw seam lines on the wrong sides of the squares. These units can then be easily hand sewn in rows.

SPEED PIECING TECHNIQUES
Strip piecing

To strip piece four-patch blocks, two strips of different fabrics, usually one light and one dark, are cut in equal widths. The strips are then sewn together lengthwise. Press seam allowances toward the darker fabric. Cut the joined strips into slices the same width as the original strips. The resulting units are then sewn in pairs to form a checkerboard effect (Figure 3–4).

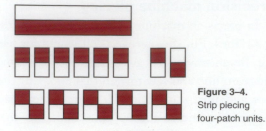

Figure 3–4.
Strip piecing
four-patch units.

Nine-patch blocks are made in the same way, except three strips of fabric are needed for each set of strips. Two dark strips are sewn with a light strip in the middle and two light strips are sewn with a dark strip in the middle. These units are then cut into slices the same width as the original strips. Three sections are sewn together in checkerboard fashion (Figure 3–5).

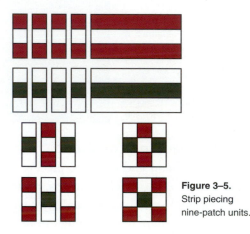

Figure 3–5.
Strip piecing
nine-patch units.

Half-square triangles

Templates. There are several different ways to form half-square triangles. A simple half-square triangle template can be made and traced on the wrong side of the fabric. Templates for machine piecing should include the ¼" seam allowance.

Rotary cutting. To make half-square triangles, rotary cut a fabric square ⅞" larger (for seam allowances) than the finished size of the triangle's short sides. The most efficient way to do this is to cut strips of fabric the needed width and then cut the strips into squares. Cut the squares diagonally, forming two half-square triangles from each one (Figure 3–6). A dark and a light half-square triangle are then sewn together to form a half-square unit.

Figure 3–6.
To make half-square triangles, cut strips into squares
and cut the squares in half diagonally.

Half-square sheets. Specially marked sheets, available at quilt shops, include directions for layering, sewing, and cutting multiple half-squares of various sizes. After the squares are sewn and cut, following the directions on the sheets, the paper is removed.

Bias half-squares. The bias-strip method is another efficient way to make a lot of half-square units. In this method, two contrasting fabrics are layered right side up and cut into 45-degree bias strips the width needed (Figure 3–7a). The strips are then arranged in two sets of alternating colors. The strips in each set are sewn together with a ¼" seam allowance (Figure 3–7b). Be careful not to stretch the bias edges. When all the strips have been sewn, two squares are formed. Each has two relatively straight edges and two jagged edges. The half-squares are cut to the size unit needed by using a rotary cutter and a square ruler with a marked 45-degree angle (Figure 3–7c).

Figure 3–7. Bias half-squares:
(a) Cut two fabric layers,
a light and a dark, into bias strips.

(b) Sew strips together, alternating colors.

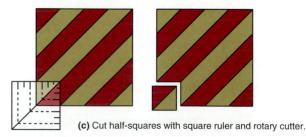

(c) Cut half-squares with square ruler and rotary cutter.

Quarter-square triangles

A quarter-square triangle is formed when a square is cut diagonally in both directions. Though these triangles look the same as half-square triangles, a half-square triangle has the straight of grain on the two short sides. A quarter-square triangle has the straight of grain on the long side. To rotary cut quarter-square triangles, add 1¼" for seam allowances to the finished length of the long side of the triangle. Cut a square this size, and slice it diagonally in both directions (Figure 3–8).

Figure 3–8.
Quarter-square triangles.

Some of the quilts in this book will need a two-color quarter-square unit. These units are most easily made by cutting half-square triangles from two contrasting fabrics and sewing them together along one of the short sides (Figure 3–9).

Figure 3–9.
Sew two half-square triangles together to make a quarter-square unit.

PAPER-PIECING BASICS

Some of the projects in this book can be made by using paper-piecing techniques. To paper piece, the sewing is done on the side of the paper with the line drawing of the block. The fabrics are placed on the other side of the paper, with at least a ¼" seam allowance extending beyond the sewing line. The wrong side of the fabric will be toward the paper when finished. This may seem tricky at first, but with a little practice, many people adopt this as their preferred way of sewing any pattern that can be adapted to this method.

The key to this method is to precut the shape needed with a larger than usual seam allowance. Odd angles can be cut by placing the fabric wrong side up, parallel to, but below the paper design. With a ruler placed along the angle on the paper and also crossing the fabric, cut the angle with a rotary cutter (Figure 3–10).

Some of the patterns must be paper-pieced in sections, and then the sections are sewn together. In some of the trees, the trunk unit can be strip pieced and sewn to the paper-pieced section (Figure 3–11).

APPLIQUÉ TECHNIQUES

There are a variety of ways to appliqué fabrics. The needle-turn method can be used with any of the appliqué patterns in this book.

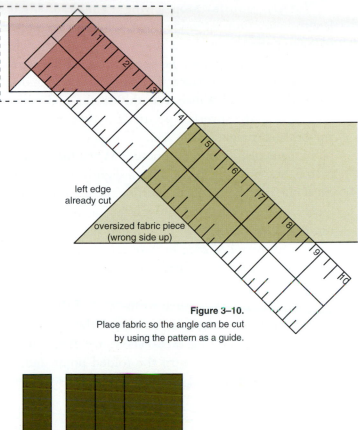

Figure 3–10.
Place fabric so the angle can be cut by using the pattern as a guide.

left edge already cut

oversized fabric piece (wrong side up)

Figure 3–11.
Strip-pieced trunk units.

Needle-turn appliqué

Draw the shape on the right side of the fabric. Cut around the shape ⅛"–¼" outside the drawn line. This allowance is swept under with the side of the needle, one or two stitch lengths ahead of the stitching. Make sure the pencil line is swept under where it won't be seen. Stitches should be approximately ¹⁄₁₆"–⅛" apart with a one- or two-thread bite into the appliqué "roll line" (Figure 3–12). The thread used should be fine and in a color that matches or blends with the fabric being appliquéd rather than the background.

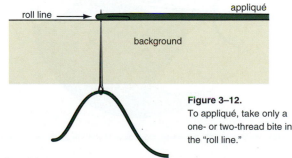

roll line

appliqué

background

Figure 3–12.
To appliqué, take only a one- or two-thread bite in the "roll line."

Inside points. Stop sewing a couple of stitch lengths away from an inside point. Clip into the point without cutting through the drawn line. Using the side of the needle, sweep from the opposite side of the point toward the last stitch taken. This motion should move all of the seam allowance smoothly to the underside, leaving a sharp inverted point. If it does not look smooth and straight, sweep again. You may need to do a bit of manipulating with your needle. When the roll line is straight, sew to the point. Take a slightly deeper than usual bite into the appliqué, inserting the needle slightly under the rolled edge and through the background fabric. Bring the needle back up through the background fabric and the rolled edge to form the start of the first stitch on the other side of the point (Figure 3–13).

Outside points. Stitch to the end of the drawn line. With the needle, turn under just the point at a slight angle. Trim off the excess allowance. Again, with the side of the needle, turn the folded point under, smoothing the rolled edge with the needle as you go.

Use the side of the needle to sweep the allowance under on the other side of the point. With a small tug on the thread, sharpen the folded point. Continue to sweep under the allowance and sew the other side of the point (Figure 3–14 on the facing page).

QUILT ASSEMBLY
Quilt settings

Blocks can be set together in a number of ways to form a quilt top. They can simply be placed next to each other, sashing can be used to separate them, or they can be combined with alternate blocks that are either a different block pattern or plain fabric. Check the size of each block for accuracy before sewing them together or adding sashing.

Borders

Once the blocks are set together, borders may be added. Borders can be made from plain strips of fabric, or they can be pieced or appliquéd. Border corners can be mitered, set square, or sewn with corner squares. In

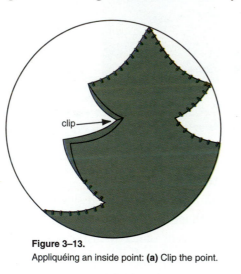

Figure 3–13.
Appliquéing an inside point: **(a)** Clip the point.

(b) Stitch to within one or two stitches of the point.

(c) Use the needle in a sweeping motion to roll the allowance under.

(d) Take a larger bite into the appliqué at the point.

Figure 3–14.
Appliquéing an outside point. **(a)** Use needle to sweep point under.

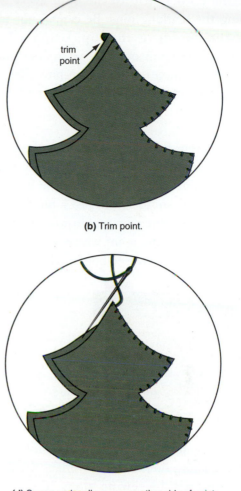

(b) Trim point.

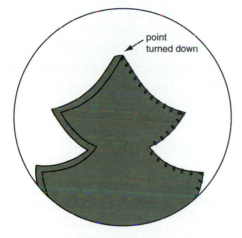

(c) Sweep point again.

(d) Sweep under allowance on other side of point.

some projects, the way the blocks are made and set together gives the impression of a border without the addition of border strips.

Before attaching a border, measure one dimension of the quilt on both edges and through the center. Repeat for the other dimension. Ideally, all three vertical measurements will be the same, and all three horizontal measurements will be the same. (Vertical and horizontal measurements will only be alike in a square quilt.) If the measurements for one dimension are different, you will need to do some adjusting in the seam allowances, taking them in or letting them out as needed. This may be a simple task or a complicated one, depending on how far off the measurements are. If you have sewn accurate ¼" seam allowances, the differences should be minute. Use the center measurements for cutting the border strips. Pin and sew the strips to the quilt, easing either the quilt top or the border strip as needed.

To sew a border with mitered corners, cut the border strips the length of the quilt, plus twice the width of the border, plus 2" for insurance. Fold the border in half crosswise to find the center. Place a pin in the allowance at this point. In addition to marking the half, you will want to mark the quarters. To find the quarter measurement, subtract the seam allowances (½") from the quilt measurement. Divide the remainder by 4. Place a pin this distance on each side of the center pin to mark the quarters. Mark the quilt top in the same way (Figure 3–15).

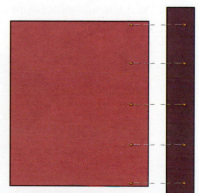

Figure 3–15.
Use pins to mark the half and quarter points and ¼" in from each end on the quilt top and border strip.

Pin the border strip to the quilt every 2" to 3", matching the marking pins. Be careful not to stretch either the border or the top. Using a ¼" seam allowance, sew from one ¼" seam-line pin to the other, easing as necessary between pins. Remove pins as you go. Do not sew beyond the pins marking the ¼" seam allowances.

When all four sides have been sewn, the corners can be mitered, as follows: Make sure everything is lying flat and smooth. At the corners, the border strips should cross one another with just a bit of extra fabric extending in each direction (approximately 1"). Mark a diagonal line from the point where the seams cross to the V formed by the crossed borders (Figure 3–16).

Figure 3–16.
Draw a diagonal line on the top border strip.

Fold the quilt diagonally from the corner, right sides together, making sure nothing overlaps the drawn line because you will be sewing along it. Carefully pin along the line without disturbing the alignment of the border strips. Stitch from the corner seams toward the outside edge, being careful not to pull or stretch this bias seam. Be sure to lock the stitches at each end.

Unfold the quilt to make sure the seam is right and that you have not sewn too deeply into the corner, creating a pleat. All three seam lines coming into the corner should end at exactly the same point. When you are sure the seam is correct, trim the excess fabric from the borders, leaving ¼" seam allowances (Figure 3–17). Press the allowances open. Repeat for the other three corners.

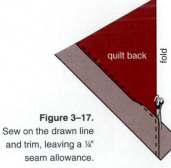

quilt back   fold

Figure 3–17.
Sew on the drawn line and trim, leaving a ¼" seam allowance.

Mark quilting lines before layering and basting. Once the layering is done, it is difficult to mark accurately on the soft surface.

Basting techniques

For hand quilting, the three layers of the quilt sandwich need to be hand basted together. Use either a basting frame or flat surface for this process. First, lay the backing down, wrong side up, and smooth it. If using a basting frame, carefully thumbtack it to the wooden frame. If using the floor or tables pushed together, tape the backing to the surface. Center the batting on top of the backing and smooth it carefully. Finally, center the quilt top on the batting, right side up, making sure it is square and straight.

Starting in the center, first divide the quilt into quadrants by basting across it horizontally and vertically. Then baste a grid 4"–6" apart in horizontal and vertical rows, working a quarter of the quilt at the time. The last row of stitches should be ¼" away from the edge of the quilt top.

Release the quilt from the frame, table, or floor. Fold excess backing over the raw edges of the batting, just covering the edges of the quilt top, and baste. Covering the edges will keep the batting and the quilt top edge from fraying during quilting.

For machine quilting, the stretching, layering and centering are the same as for hand quilting. Instead of using a needle and basting thread, however, small safety pins made specifically for machine quilting can be used to hold the three layers together. Pins need to be placed in a grid approximately every 4". The special bent safety pins are easier to use for this purpose.

Once the quilting has been completed, straighten and square the quilt and cut off the excess batting and backing. Wide rotary rulers laid end to end will help with this process. A large square ruler or a carpenter's "L" is helpful at the corners. Be sure to leave a sufficient amount of batting beyond the quilt edges to fill the binding.

Binding raw edges

A narrow binding can be used on most quilts. Cut enough fabric strips 1¾" to 2½" wide, either on the straight of grain or the bias, to equal the total of the four sides of the quilt plus about a foot. Join the strips together with diagonal seams (Figure 3–18). Trim the seam allowances to ¼" and press them open. When all the strips have been joined, cut the beginning end of the continuous strip at a 45-degree angle and fold the strip in half, wrong sides together, along its entire length.

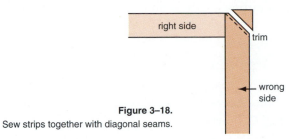

Figure 3–18.
Sew strips together with diagonal seams.

Beginning about 14" from a corner, lay the binding along the edge of the quilt, matching the raw edges of the binding to the raw edge of the quilt top. In the corner, place a pin ¼" away from the edge to indicate the seam line for the next side of the quilt (Figure 3–19a). Leaving about 8" of the binding unsewn, begin sewing at least 6" from the corner. Use a walking foot and a ¼" seam allowance to sew just to the pin. End with three or four backstitches.

Clip the threads and take the quilt away from the machine. Fold the binding straight up, creating a diagonal fold (Figure 3–19b). Bring the binding straight down along the next side of the quilt to be sewn (Figure 3–19c).

Figure 3–19.
Sewing binding to quilt front:
(a) Sew to the pin at the ¼" mark.

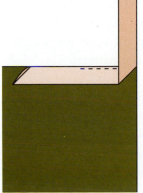

(b) Fold binding up.

(c) Fold binding down along the next edge of the quilt.

Measure the quilt through the center and subtract ¼" to find out how long the binding strip needs to be for the next side. Measure the binding from the folded corner and place a pin to mark the correct length. Pin the binding to the quilt, ¼" from the edge, every 2"–3" between the fold and the ending pin. Put the quilt back under the presser foot and sew from the binding fold to the pin, locking the stitches at both ends. Repeat these steps at each corner.

For the last side, measure carefully, subtracting the 14" for the first end of the binding. *Do not cut yet.* Stitch until you are about 6" from the first end. Smooth the tail end on top of the first end. leaving at least a 5" overlap, then cut the tail end.

Place the tail end inside the folded first end and mark the leading edge of the first end on the tail end (Figure 3–20a). To allow for the two seam allowances, measure ½" to the right of the line and draw a second 45-degree line on the tail end. *Do not cut yet.* Unfold both ends. Finish drawing the two lines across the binding, making sure the angles are going the same direction as the starting cut angle (Figure 3–20b).

Twist the first end so it is wrong side up. With right sides together, place the diagonal edge of the first end on the second drawn line. Offset the pieces approximately ¼" to accommodate seam allowances, as shown in Figure 3–20c. Pin in place. Refold the binding and smooth it to see if the binding will lie flat. *Do not cut yet.*

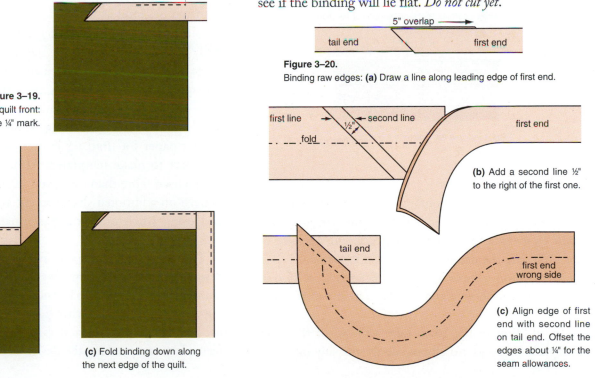

Figure 3–20.
Binding raw edges: **(a)** Draw a line along leading edge of first end.

(b) Add a second line ½" to the right of the first one.

(c) Align edge of first end with second line on tail end. Offset the edges about ¼" for the seam allowances.

Stitch the two ends together with a ¼" seam allowance, as shown in the figure. Refold and smooth the binding in place again. If it fits, you can cut the tail end, leaving a ¼" seam allowance. If not, adjust as necessary and resew before cutting. Press the seam allowances open. Refold the binding and finish sewing it to the quilt.

Fold the binding to the back of the quilt, covering the raw edges and mitering the corners, Sew the binding to the back by hand with an invisible appliqué stitch. Be sure to sew the mitered corners closed.

Hanging sleeve

Cut a strip of fabric 8½" wide by the width of the quilt. Make narrow hems on each end of the strip. Fold the strip in half lengthwise, wrong sides together (Figure 3–21a). Stitch the entire length with a ¼" seam allowance. Rotate the seam to the center of the back, where it can't be seen, and press the allowances open. Pin the sleeve on the back of the quilt, just below the binding on the top edge of the quilt. Appliqué the sleeve in place, making sure none of the stitches go through to the front of the quilt (Figure 3–21b).

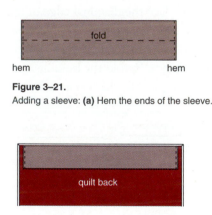

Figure 3–21.
Adding a sleeve: **(a)** Hem the ends of the sleeve.

(b) Hand sew the sleeve to the quilt back.

Creating labels

Prepare a label that contains at least your name, the place the quilt was made, and the date. You may also want to include the name of the recipient, the size of the quilt, and the name of the quilt, if it has one. Labels can range from simple appliquéd rectangles, written in fabric pen, to elaborate affairs created in any medium.

In addition to the label, take a photo of the quilt and place it in a photo album, along with any informa-

tion you may need later or that you would like to pass on to future generations. Help stamp out the words "Maker Anonymous!"

BLOCK DRAFTING

If you want to change the size of a block to fit your needs, drafting is easy to do with the following supplies:

> Pencil choices
>   mechanical pencil with .05mm lead
>   no. 2 pencil and sharpener
> Paper choices
>   graph paper
>   newsprint
>   freezer paper
>   tracing paper
> Drafting triangle
> Clear plastic or metal ruler
> Computer design programs (optional, but nice to have)

Mechanical pencils, with .05mm lead, are the easiest tools to use for drafting. The fine point aids in making drafting lines more accurate. **No. 2 pencils** can be used; however, they must be sharpened often.

Many people like to use **graph paper** for drafting designs. There are many different sizes and divisions available. As long as the design being drafted is easily divisible by the units in the graph paper, this works well. When drafting a block size in which the design lines fall between the graph paper lines, plain **newsprint**, **freezer paper**, or even **tracing paper** may work better. Drawing design lines between the graph lines can become confusing. One benefit of using **freezer paper** for drafting is that the drawing can be cut apart to make templates. Although freezer paper can be used more than once, you may want to trace the pattern on additional sheets to cut apart for templates and keep a whole one for a master pattern.

Tracing paper is also useful in planning quilting designs. By placing tracing paper over a finished block or quilt, quilting designs can be tried without actually quilting the fabric. These tracing paper designs can then be used as master patterns and can be transferred to template plastic for marking the design on the finished top.

Drafting triangles can be purchased with either a 60-degree angle or a 45-degree angle. One of the angles on the rulers is 90 degrees. To use this tool to make a square, draw a line the size of the square desired. Align the base of the drafting triangle with the drawn line and draw the second side of the square (Figure 3–22a). Turn the drafting triangle over to draw the third side (Figure 3–22b). Mark the square's measurements on the two sides of the square and use a ruler to connect the marks, completing the square (Figure 3–22c).

Figure 3–22.
Drafting an accurate square: **(a)** Align drafting triangle with first side of square to draw second side.

(b) Reverse triangle for third side.

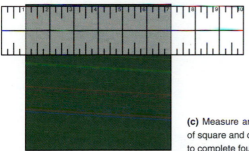

(c) Measure and mark sides of square and connect marks to complete fourth side.

Clear acrylic rulers, the same rulers used for rotary cutting, or metal rulers from the drafting supply area of an office supply store are needed for accurately measuring the various divisions when drafting a block. The inexpensive wood or plastic rulers often used by students are hard to use and will not give the accuracy needed. The ability to see through the acrylic ruler is a real advantage.

Computer programs are available for drafting blocks. Some programs were created especially for quiltmaking, and others are general drawing programs. In Chapter One, the various grids used for Pine Tree blocks are shown. While these grids range from 5 to 14 divisions, you may occasionally need a block in a size that is not easily divided by the number of units printed on the grid paper.

For example, for an 8" tree block or any other block that has a grid of five divisions, you would need to cut half-square triangles that finish 1.6". This is not an easy task because rulers are not marked for this odd size.

There are several options for solving this problem. You can choose a different block with a grid of eight. You can use a computer program to electronically change the size of the block, assuming the block is already in the program or you are willing to draft it in the program. (Occasionally, depending on your printer, the templates printed are not accurate, and it is disheartening to discover this after attempting to sew the block together.) The third option is to learn to draft the block by using a method that will allow for making accurate templates no matter the size of the block. The following method can be used with any grid for any block you want to resize, and you won't be restricted by the markings on your ruler.

DRAFTING ODD-SIZED BLOCKS

To draft a block, you will need only four pieces of equipment: paper (freezer paper can be used), a mechanical pencil with a .05 lead, a ruler longer than the square to be divided, and a drafting triangle. Freezer paper is available in the supermarket, and the other items are readily available in office supply stores. The ruler may be the same one used for rotary cutting.

1. To divide an 8" block into five equal divisions, first draft an 8" square as described previously and shown in Figure 3–22.

2. This is where the magic begins. Angle the ruler from one corner of the drawn square, making sure the zero is at the corner. Rotate the ruler until it crosses the opposite side of the square at a measurement divis-

ible by the number of divisions needed. In this case, 10" is easily divisible by five.

3. Make a dot at 2", 4", 6", and 8" to divide the block into five equal divisions (Figure 3–23).

4. Use the triangle placed on the base line to draw divisions parallel to the sides of the square (Figure 3–24).

5. Rotate the square a quarter turn and repeat steps 2–4 to create 25 squares to complete a grid with five divisions (Figure 3–25).

6. Follow the block design to fill in the half-square triangles and trunk pieces.

Occasionally, a block may be so small that you will need to extend the lines beyond the edges of the block to be able to use this method (Figure 3–26).

After the block has been drafted you can use it to make hand- or machine-piecing templates.

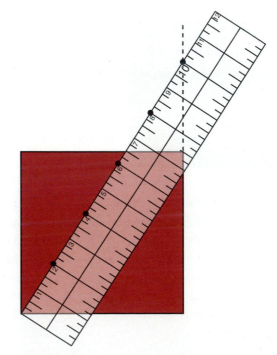

Figure 3–25.
Repeat steps 2–4 to draw lines in the other direction.

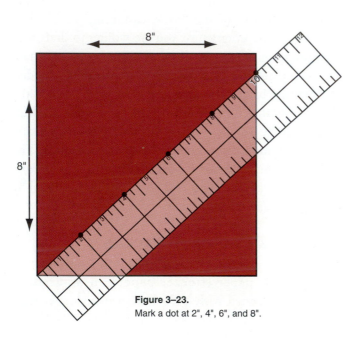

Figure 3–23.
Mark a dot at 2", 4", 6", and 8".

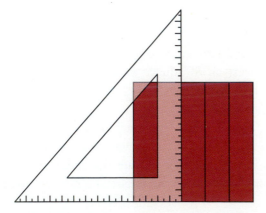

Figure 3–24.
Use the marks to draw equal divisions across the square.

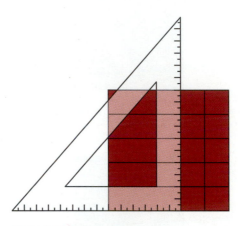

Figure 3–26.
Draw a line extending the side of the square, if needed to accommodate the ruler.

Chapter 4

Pine Tree
Quilt Projects

A Small Forest

Smaller quilt: 18½" x18½"
Larger quilt: 28" x 28"

Finished block: 4" x 4"
Finished block: 6" x 6"

A SMALL FOREST (28" x 28") by Marian Gillian.
This quick and easy paper-foundation-pieced project comes in
two sizes for wallhangings. With only five trees, it would indeed be a very small forest.

FABRIC REQUIREMENTS AND CUTTING

Fabrics*	Yards	Pieces
Background	¼ (⅓)	
corner triangles		2 squares 3¾" (5¼")
side triangles		1 square 7" (9¾")
Brown: trunks	scrap	1 square 6" (8")
Accent:	⅓ (½)	
border 1		4 strips 1½" x 16"
		(4 strips 2" x 22½")
binding		3 (4) strips 1¾" x 42"
Green: trees	⅛ (¼) ea.	
(choose 5 different greens)		—
Border 2	½ (¾)	4 strips 3" x 21"
		(4 strips 4½" x 30")
Backing square	¾ (1)	1 square 22" (31")
Batting square	—	1 square 22" (31")

*Yardage based on 42"-wide fabric. Larger quilt given in parentheses.

PINE TREE BLOCKS

1. Make five copies of the 4" or 6" tree pattern on a photo copier or trace the pattern on a paper suitable for foundations.

2. Construct five paper-foundation pieced blocks according to the general directions on page 35.

QUILT ASSEMBLY

3. Follow the Quilt Assembly diagram (Figure 4–1) to sew the blocks and setting triangles in diagonal rows. Sew the rows together.

4. Sew the border-1 strips to all four sides of the quilt and miter the corners. Repeat for border 2.

5. Layer the backing, batting, and quilt top. Baste and quilt as desired. In-the-ditch quilting was used around the blocks and the background patches next to the trunks. The corner and side triangles were quilted free-hand.

6. Following directions on page 38–40, bind the raw edges of the quilt.

Figure 4–1.
Quilt assembly.

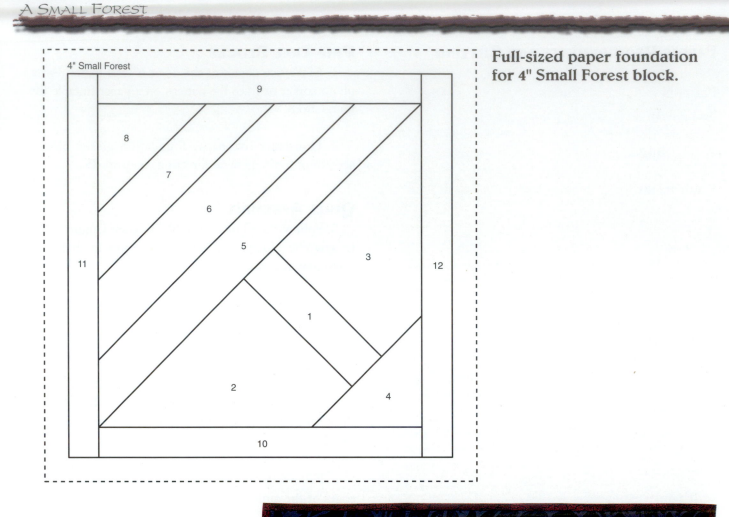

4" Small Forest

Full-sized paper foundation for 4" Small Forest block.

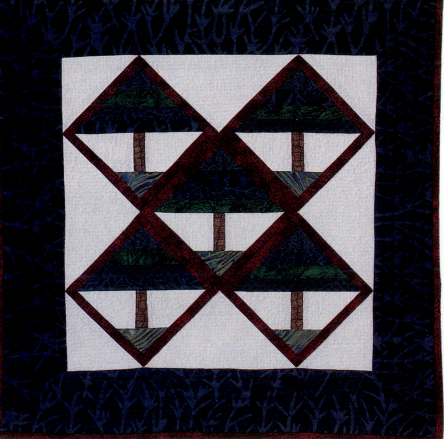

A SMALL FOREST by the author, 16" x 16".
The author eliminated Border 1 in this version.

Full-sized paper foundation for 6" Small Forest block.

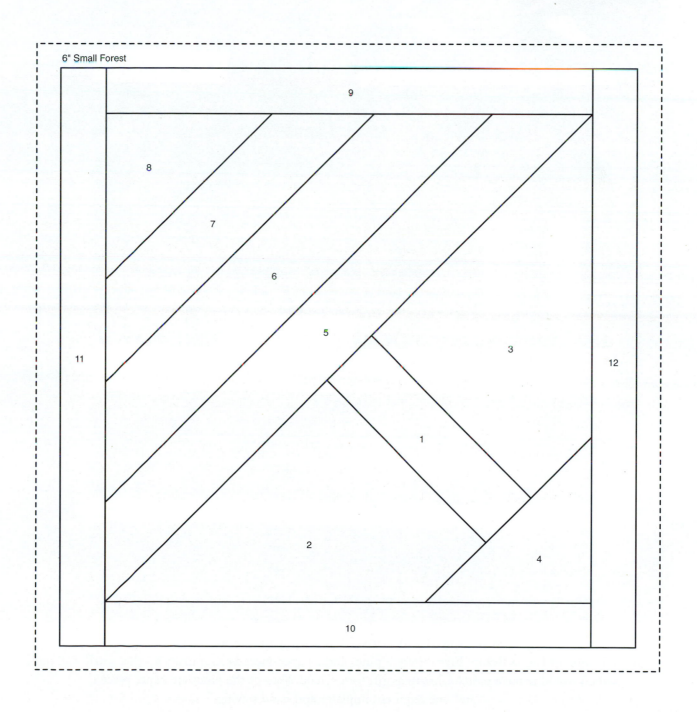

6" Small Forest

9

8

7

6

5

3

11

12

1

2

4

10

Cabin in the Woods

Quilt: 24" x 25"
Finished blocks: 1 cabin 8" x 8"
2 pines 4" x 8" (two varieties)
6 pines 4" x 4" (three varieties)

CABIN IN THE WOODS (24" x 25") by the author.
In the collection of Linda Braun. Five different pines and a paper-pieced cabin make up this small wall quilt
which would make a pretty Christmas gift for a friend. Four of the pines are paper pieced,
and one requires templates and hand sewing.

FABRIC REQUIREMENTS AND CUTTING

Fabrics*	Yards	Pieces
Green: branches (the more variety the better)	scraps	—
Red: cabin, chimneys	scraps	—
Yellow: windows	scraps	—
Brown: trunks	scraps	—
Black: door	scraps	—
Dark blue: roof	scraps	—
White snow: spacer	¼	1 strip 1½" x 16½"
Blue background: border	1	4 strips 4½" x 27"
Backing	⅞	1 panel 27" x 28"
Binding	¼	3 strips 2½" x 42
Batting	—	27" x 28"

*Yardage based on 42"-wide fabric.

BLOCK ASSEMBLY

The cabin and all the trees, except tree E, are paper-foundation pieced in sections. The sections are then joined. Make four of tree A, one of tree B, two of tree C, two of tree D, and one Cabin.

Tree E

The trunk section can be foundation paper pieced, but you will need to make individual freezer-paper templates for the curved pieces, as follows:

1. Trace the tree sections, including the hatch marks, on the dull side of a piece of freezer paper.

2. Before you are ready to sew, cut the freezer-paper pattern for one section to make templates for the curved patches. Leave the rest of the sections intact until you're ready to piece them. This way will be less confusing.

3. Iron the freezer paper templates to the wrong sides of the appropriate fabrics.

4. Leaving a ¼" seam allowance, by eye, cut around the templates. Leave the templates in place. It's easiest to piece the tight curves by hand sewing rather than using a machine.

5. Pin tree pieces 1 and 2, right sides together. Be sure to place pins at each point and carefully match the hatch marks on the templates. Use a sufficient number of pins to distribute the fullness evenly between the pin at the beginning edge, the pin at the hatch mark, and the pin at the end of the stitching line.

6. Sew the pieces together by using the edge of the freezer paper as a seam guide. Sew as close to the freezer paper as possible.

7. Stitch the blue "sky" pieces to each side of tree-branch unit, carefully matching the hatch marks and easing fullness as before. Repeat with the remaining two tree sections.

8. The trunk section can be made with templates, or it can be paper-pieced. Repeat the steps to make the second tree.

QUILT ASSEMBLY

9. Join blocks into sections as shown in the Quilt Assembly diagram (Figure 4–2 on the following page). Sew the sections together to form the upper portion of the quilt. Sew the spacer strip to the bottom of the upper portion. Add the bottom row of trees to the quilt.

10. Stitch the four border strips to the quilt and follow the directions on pages 36–38 to miter the corners.

11. Layer the top, batting, and backing. Baste and quilt as desired. In the quilt in the photo, all the shapes in the cabin and trees were outlined with in-the-ditch quilting. Wavy lines representing snow drifts were quilted in the white areas. Side by side Christmas tree shapes were quilted in the border.

12. Bind the quilt, following directions on pages 38–40.

Figure 4–2.
Quilt assembly.

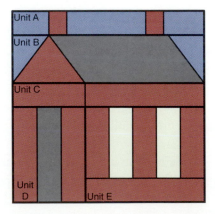

Cabin block

Full-sized paper foundations for 8" Cabin block.

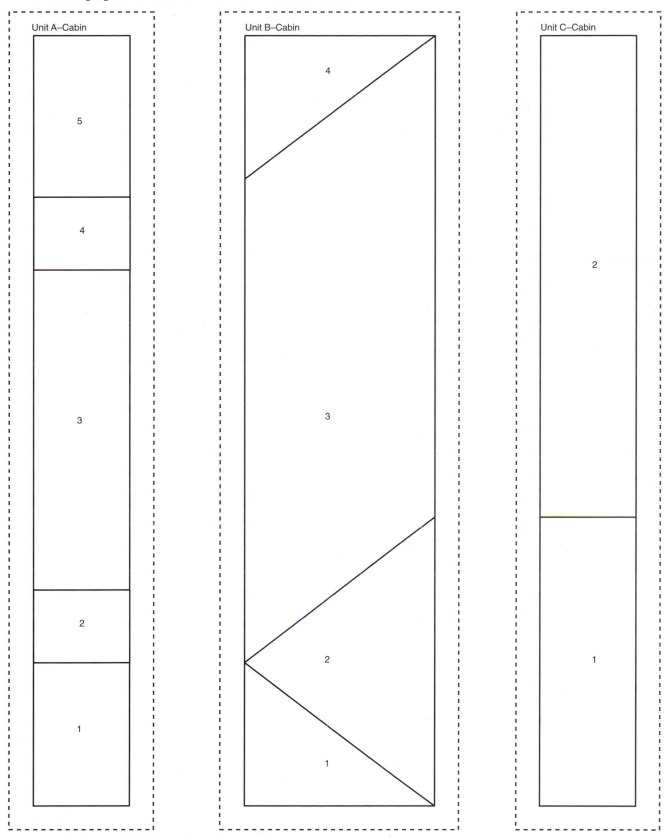

Pattern is reversed for placing fabric underneath. The lines on the pattern are sewing lines.

8" Cabin block continued

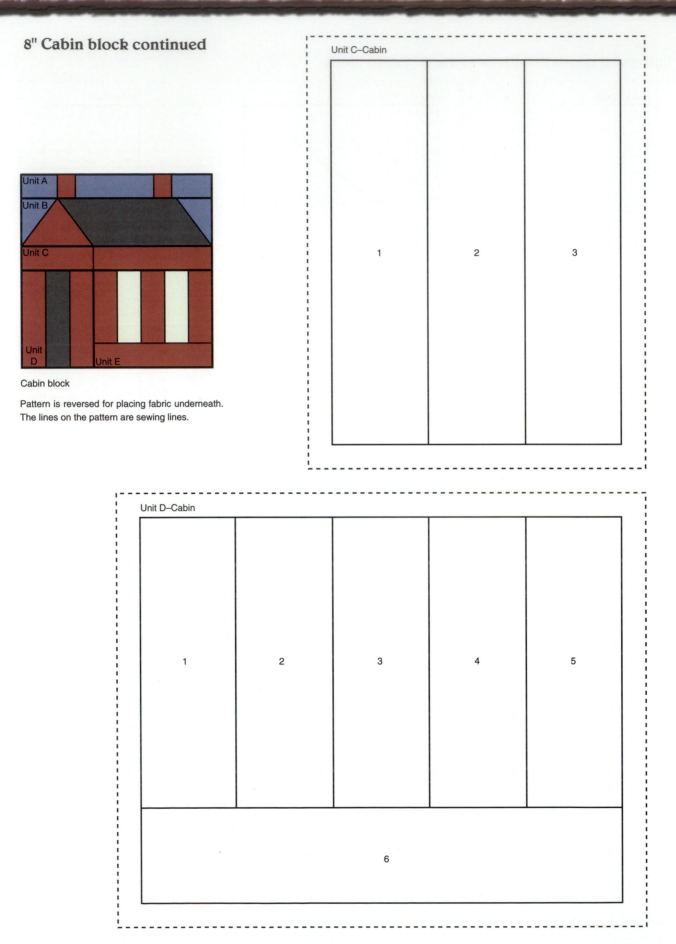

Cabin block

Pattern is reversed for placing fabric underneath.
The lines on the pattern are sewing lines.

Unit C–Cabin

| 1 | 2 | 3 |

Unit D–Cabin

| 1 | 2 | 3 | 4 | 5 |

6

Full-sized paper foundations for Tree blocks A and C.

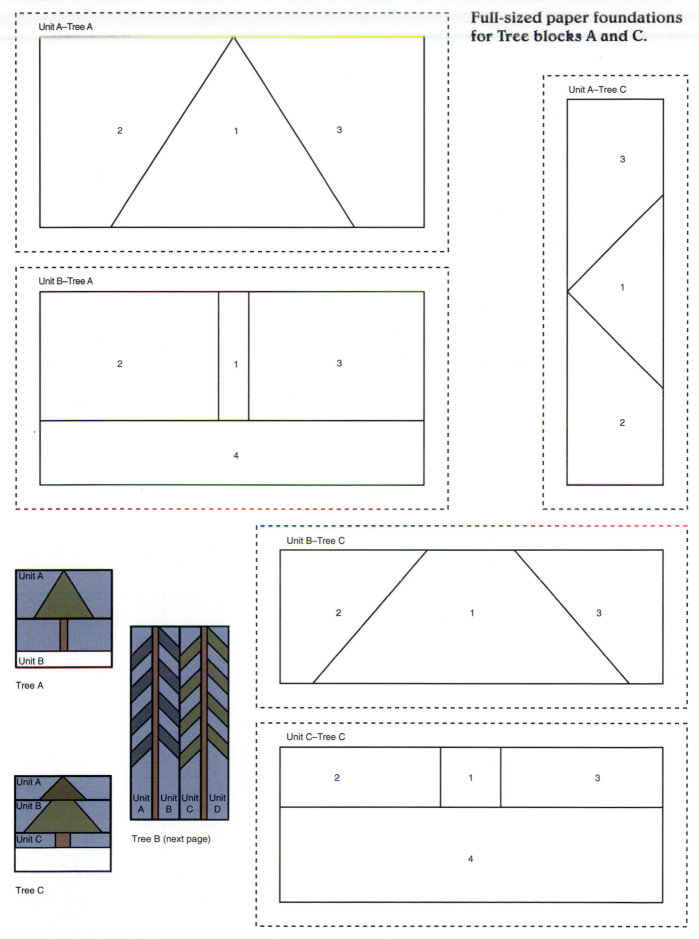

Unit A–Tree A

2   1   3

Unit B–Tree A

2   1   3

4

Unit A–Tree C

3

1

2

Unit B–Tree C

2   1   3

Unit C–Tree C

2   1   3

4

Unit A
Unit B

Tree A

Unit A
Unit B
Unit C

Tree C

Unit A   Unit B   Unit C   Unit D

Tree B (next page)

Full-sized paper foundations for Tree B.

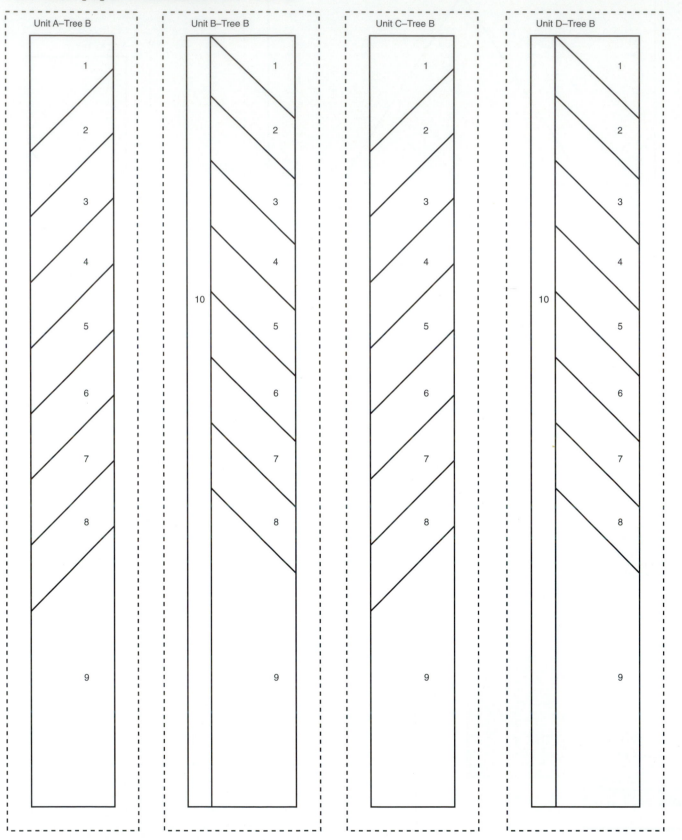

Full-sized paper foundations for Tree D.

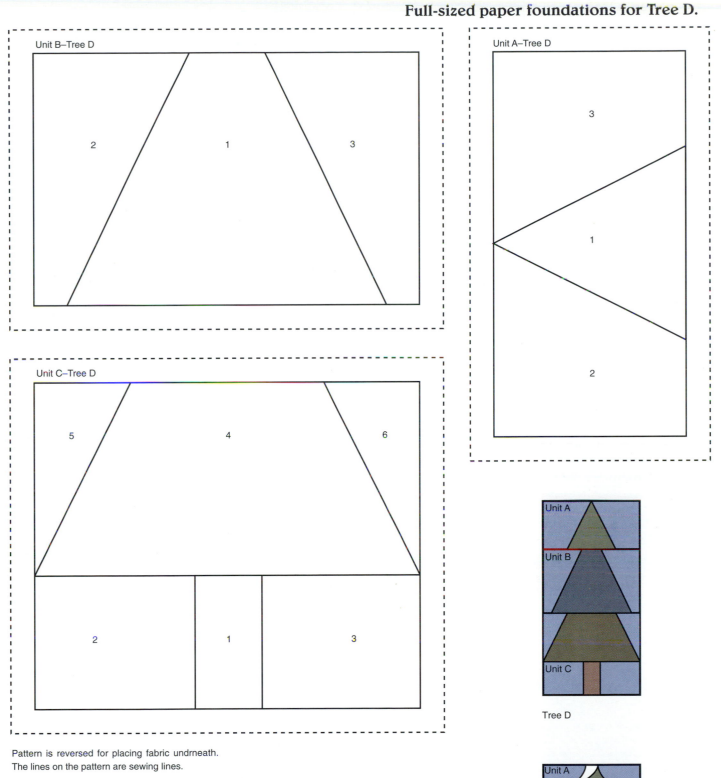

Unit B–Tree D

2   1   3

Unit A–Tree D

3

1

2

Unit C–Tree D

5   4   6

2   1   3

Pattern is reversed for placing fabric undrneath.
The lines on the pattern are sewing lines.

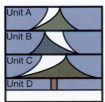

Unit A

Unit B

Unit C

Tree D

Unit A
Unit B
Unit C
Unit D

Tree E (next page)

Full-sized paper foundations for Tree E.

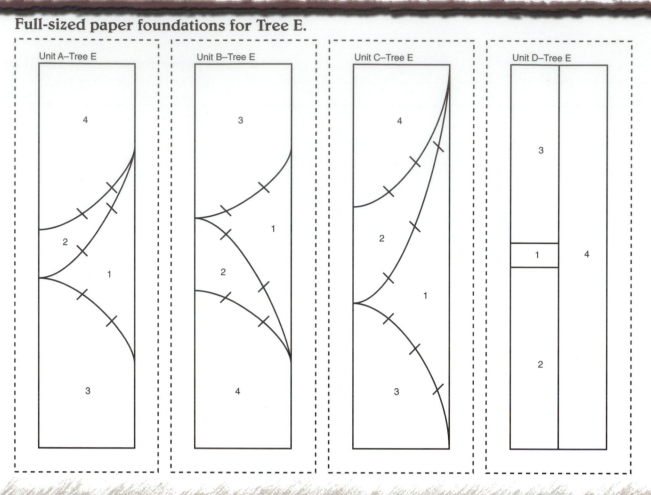

| Unit A–Tree E | Unit B–Tree E | Unit C–Tree E | Unit D–Tree E |

PINE DINING Place Mats

Fabric Requirements and Cutting

Fabrics*	Yards	Pieces
Green: branches	scraps	—
Brown: trunks	scraps	—
Background:	½	
trees, both sides		2 squares 12½" x 12½"
or trees, one side		2 rectangles 15½" x 12½"
Backing	½	2 rectangles 21" x 15"
Binding	⅓	4 strips 1¾" x 42"
Batting	—	2 rectangles 21" x 15"

*Amounts are for two place mats. Yardage based on 42"-wide fabric.

Mat Assembly

1. All tree designs are 3" wide by 3", 4", or 6" tall. Choose two, three, or four blocks of the same or different designs. Photocopy or trace the patterns. Construct the number of paper-pieced trees needed.

2. Sew vertical rows of blocks to equal 12½" tall, including seam allowances. Sew the rows on the left or right side of the 15½" x 12½" rectangle or on both sides of the 12½" x 12½" square (Figure 4–3).

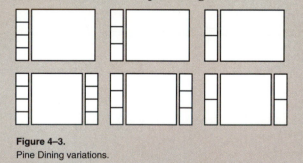

Figure 4–3.
Pine Dining variations.

3. Layer the backing, batting, and place-mat top. Baste with thread or pins. Quilt as desired. The mats on pages 57 and 58 were quilted in the ditch to outline the trees. The bodies of the place mats were quilted in a 1" cross hatch.

4. Bind edges of the place mat (described on pages 38–40).

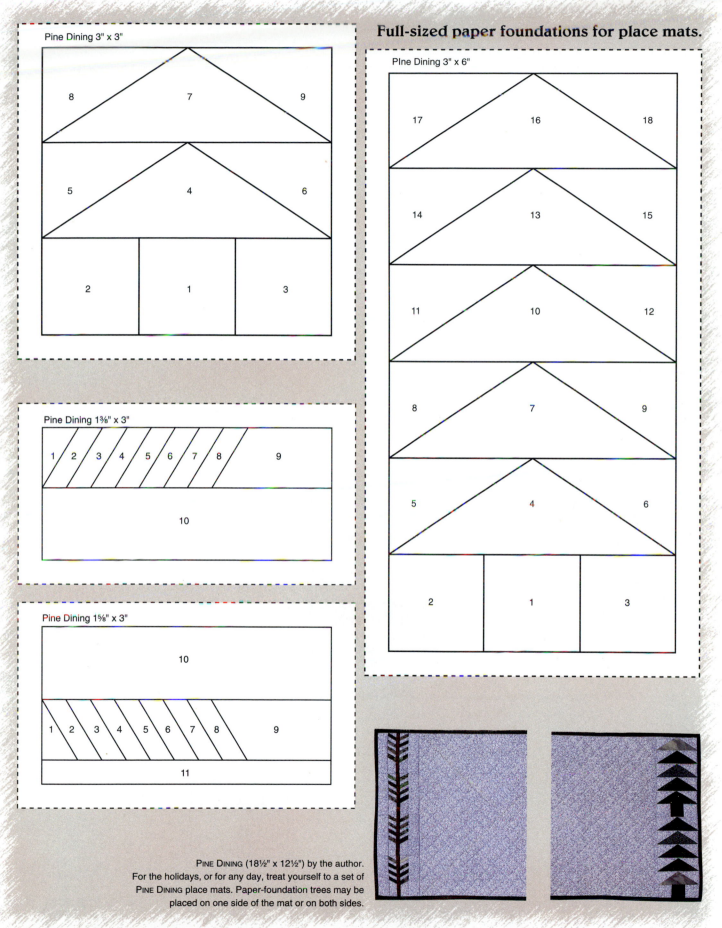

Full-sized paper foundations for place mats.

Pine Dining 3" x 3"

Pine Dining 3" x 6"

Pine Dining 1⅜" x 3"

Pine Dining 1⅝" x 3"

PINE DINING (18½" x 12½") by the author.
For the holidays, or for any day, treat yourself to a set of
PINE DINING place mats. Paper-foundation trees may be
placed on one side of the mat or on both sides.

Full-sized paper foundations for place mats.

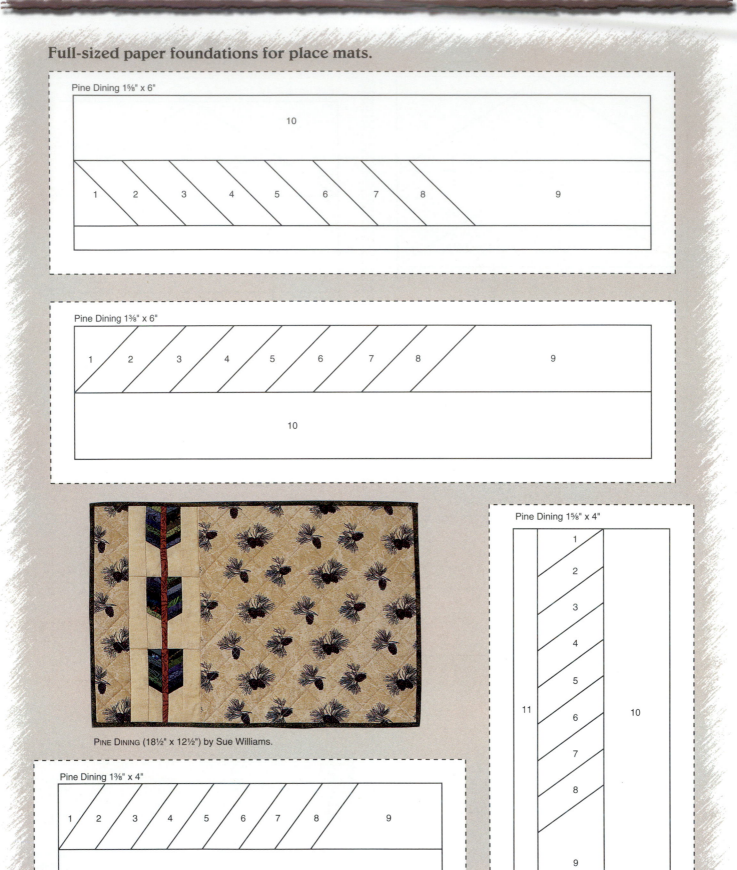

Pine Dining 1⅝" x 6"

				10				

| 1 | 2 | 3 | 4 | 5 | 6 | 7 | 8 | 9 |

Pine Dining 1⅜" x 6"

| 1 | 2 | 3 | 4 | 5 | 6 | 7 | 8 | 9 |

| | | | | 10 | | | | |

PINE DINING (18½" x 12½") by Sue Williams.

Pine Dining 1⅝" x 4"

| 11 | 1 2 3 4 5 6 7 8 9 | 10 |

Pine Dining 1⅜" x 4"

| 1 | 2 | 3 | 4 | 5 | 6 | 7 | 8 | 9 |

| 10 |

Quilt: 48" x 48"
Finished blocks:
4 Pine in the Forest 12" x 12"   4 Birds in the Pine 12" x 12"
5 Eight-Pointed Stars 4" x 4"   44 Pine in the Forest 4" x 4"
                                        4 Plain Squares 4" x 4"

Explore Arizona

EXPLORE ARIZONA (47" x 47") by Joyce Buchberger.
The quiltmaker was given these block designs and asked to use purple (one of her favorite colors) in the quilt.
Inspired by the varied terrain in her home state of Arizona, she used Southwestern colors from the desert
and greens from the mountain pines. Use a variety of green fabrics, including different values and textures
for the branches. For the trunk units, use the same green background in the 4" and in the 12" blocks.
Select a variety of purples for the mountains in the trunk units.

FABRIC REQUIREMENTS AND CUTTING

Fabrics*	Yards	Patches
Southwest print:	1	
sky		4 K, 4 Kr
		4 squares 4½" x 4½"
border 2		4 strips 1¾" x 42"
Light purple: sky	⅜	(4" Pine in the Forest)
Medium purple: sky	½	8 A, 8 F
Purple: mountains	scraps	16 B
Brown: trunks	¼	8 D
Green: branches	scraps	8 B, 80 E, 4 G, 4 H, 4 I, 4 J
Green:	¾	
trunk-unit background		16 A, 16 C
Red: stars	⅛	40 M
Dark purple:	⅜	
star background		20 L, 20 N
border 1		4 strips 1¼" x 42"
Backing	3	2 panels 26" x 51"
Binding	½	6 strips 2½" x 42"
Batting	—	51" x 51"

*Yardage based on 42"-wide fabric.

BIRDS IN THE PINE

1. Construct 36 half-square units from light green and dark green triangles (E patches). Trim units to 2⅝" x 2⅝".

2. Using Figure 4–4 as a guide, join nine half-square units to form the block's center square on point. Make four center squares.

3. To complete a branch section, sew one purple triangle A to the left side of a green triangle B. Sew a green triangle E to the top of the A/B unit. Make a mirror-image A/B/E unit. Join these units and the F triangles to the sides of a center square. Repeat for the other center squares.

4. For a trunk section, sew one green triangle C to each side of trunk D. Join a green triangle A to a purple

triangle B. Make a mirror-image A/B unit. Sew the A/B units to the trunk unit. Make eight trunk units. Save four of the units for the Large Pine in the Forest block.

5. Join a trunk unit to the bottom edge of a branch section to complete the block. Make four Birds in the Pine blocks.

LARGE PINE IN THE FOREST

6. Following Figure 4–5, join G, H, I, and J to form the tree branches. Sew triangles K and Kr to each side.

7. Sew a trunk unit to the bottom edge of the branch section. Make four Pine in the Forest blocks.

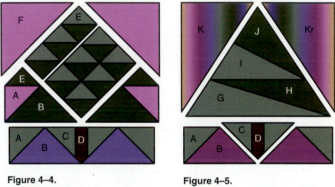

Figure 4–4.
Birds in the Pine block assembly.

Figure 4–5.
Pine in the Forest block assembly.

SMALL PINE IN THE FOREST

8. Make 44 copies of the 4" Pine in the Forest pattern. (If using a photocopier, be sure to find one that does not distort the pattern.)

9. Following the general paper-piecing instructions on page 35, construct 40 blocks with light purple backgrounds and four blocks with dark purple backgrounds in the branch sections. Set aside the four blocks with the dark purple backgrounds to use in the center of the quilt.

4" EIGHT-POINTED STAR

10. Use templates to construct this block (Figure 4–6). The measurements of the pieces are not conducive to rotary cutting. Make five blocks, as shown in Sewing an Eight-Pointed Star, page 61.

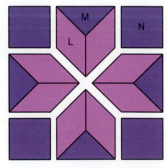

Figure 4–6.
Eight-Pointed Star block assembly.

SEWING AN EIGHT-POINTED STAR

Arrange star pieces as shown in Figure 4–7a. To sew the first unit, place the triangle on top of the left diamond, right sides together, with points offset ¼" as shown in Figure 4–7b. Sew from raw edge to raw edge. Press the seam allowance toward the triangle.

Place the second diamond, right sides together, matching the edges with the triangle (Figure 4–7c).

Turn the pieces so the triangle is on top and the previous seam is visible (Figure 4–7d). Sew from the outside point of the triangle to the seam line, making sure to lock stitches at both ends.

With the right sides of the diamonds together, match points and edges. Make sure the triangle is pulled out of the way. Sew from the edge to the previous seam and lock stitches at the end (Figure 4–7e). Press seam allowances toward the last diamond added. Sew four units (Figure 4–7f).

Match a square (N) to the diamond on the right, rights sides together. Keeping the square on top, sew from edge to edge (Figure 4–7g). Press seam allowances toward the square. Repeat three times to make quarter-blocks.

Arrange the quarter-block units as shown in Figure 4–7h. Flip the top unit down, right sides together, matching the edge of the diamond with the square. Sew the seam from the square's edge to the previous seam and lock the stitches (Figure 4–7i). Press the seam allowances toward the square.

To complete the half-block, fold the square as shown and sew the diamonds together as before (Figure 4–7j). Sew the remaining quarters together to make another half-block.

Arrange the half-blocks as shown in Figure 4–7k. With right sides together, match the top square on the right half with the diamond on the left half. Sew from the edge to the seam line and lock the stitches (Figure 4–7l). Repeat with the square and diamond on the other side of the block.

The final seam to be sewn will join the two halves diagonally. The seams should nestle together if they have all been pressed in the same direction (clockwise when looking at them from the wrong side of the block).

Before sewing this last seam, either place a pin across the center ¼" away from the edge or take a few basting stitches along the center. Check to see that the points are sharp, adjust the seams, if necessary, before sewing the final seam. When you are satisfied, sew either from seam line to seam line or from the center out to each seam line, making sure to lock stitches (Figure 4–7m). Press the final seam so it lies flat. Make 5 blocks.

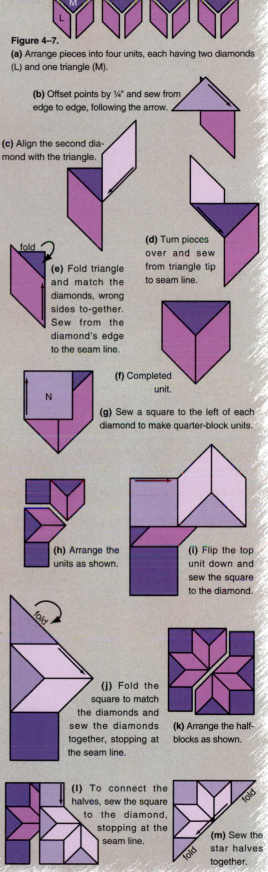

Figure 4–7.

(a) Arrange pieces into four units, each having two diamonds (L) and one triangle (M).

(b) Offset points by ¼" and sew from edge to edge, following the arrow.

(c) Align the second diamond with the triangle.

(d) Turn pieces over and sew from triangle tip to seam line.

(e) Fold triangle and match the diamonds, wrong sides to-gether. Sew from the diamond's edge to the seam line.

(f) Completed unit.

(g) Sew a square to the left of each diamond to make quarter-block units.

(h) Arrange the units as shown.

(i) Flip the top unit down and sew the square to the diamond.

(j) Fold the square to match the diamonds and sew the diamonds together, stopping at the seam line.

(k) Arrange the half-blocks as shown.

(l) To connect the halves, sew the square to the diamond, stopping at the seam line.

(m) Sew the star halves together.

CENTER BLOCK

11. To form the center block of the quilt, sew the 4½" Southwestern print squares, the four paper-pieced trees with the dark purple backgrounds, and one Eight-Pointed Star in a nine-patch formation (Figure 4–8). The center block should measure 12½", including seam allowances.

Figure 4–8.
Center block assembly.

QUILT ASSEMBLY

12. Following the quilt photo and Figure 4–9, set the 12" blocks in rows, forming a large nine patch. Sew borders 1 and 2 to the quilt, with butted corners.

13. For border 3, sew ten 4" Pine in the Forest blocks together for each side of the quilt. Sew two of the rows to opposite sides of the quilt with the tree trunks pointing outward. Sew an Eight-Pointed Star to each end of the remaining two border strips and add these borders to the quilt.

14. Layer the top, batting, and backing. Baste the layers and quilt as desired. The author quilted the miniature trees in the ditch to accentuate the fabrics. The large trees are quilted with concentric triangles, starting 1" from the edges of the pieced trees. The mountains are also quilted with echoing shapes. All background areas contain a meandering wide stipple, following the color changes in the fabrics. Follow the directions in the general instruction chapter for binding (pages 38–40).

Figure 4–9.
Quilt assembly.

Full-sized paper foundation for 4" Pine in the Forest block.

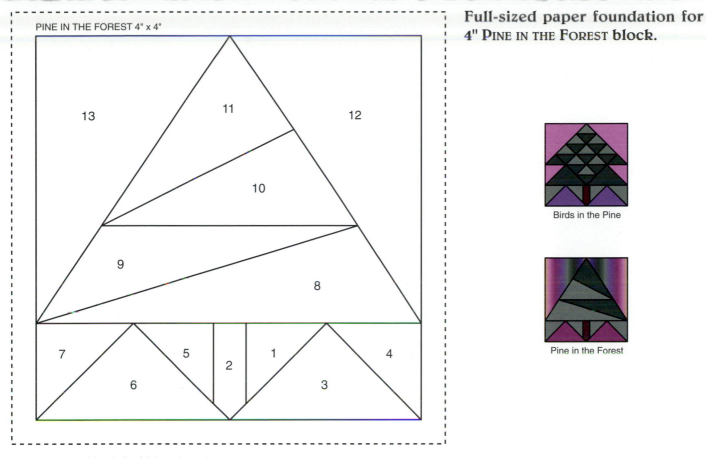

PINE IN THE FOREST 4" x 4"

Pattern is reversed for placing fabric underneath.
The lines on the pattern are sewing lines.

Birds in the Pine

Pine in the Forest

12" Birds in the Pine and Pine in the Forest patterns.

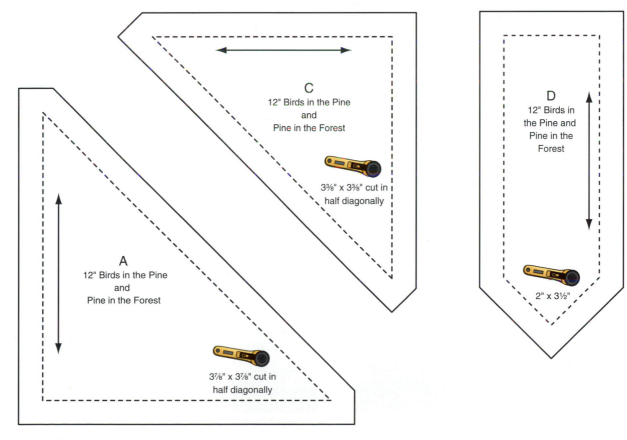

C
12" Birds in the Pine
and
Pine in the Forest

3⅜" x 3⅜" cut in
half diagonally

D
12" Birds in
the Pine and
Pine in the
Forest

2" x 3½"

A
12" Birds in the Pine
and
Pine in the Forest

3⅞" x 3⅞" cut in
half diagonally

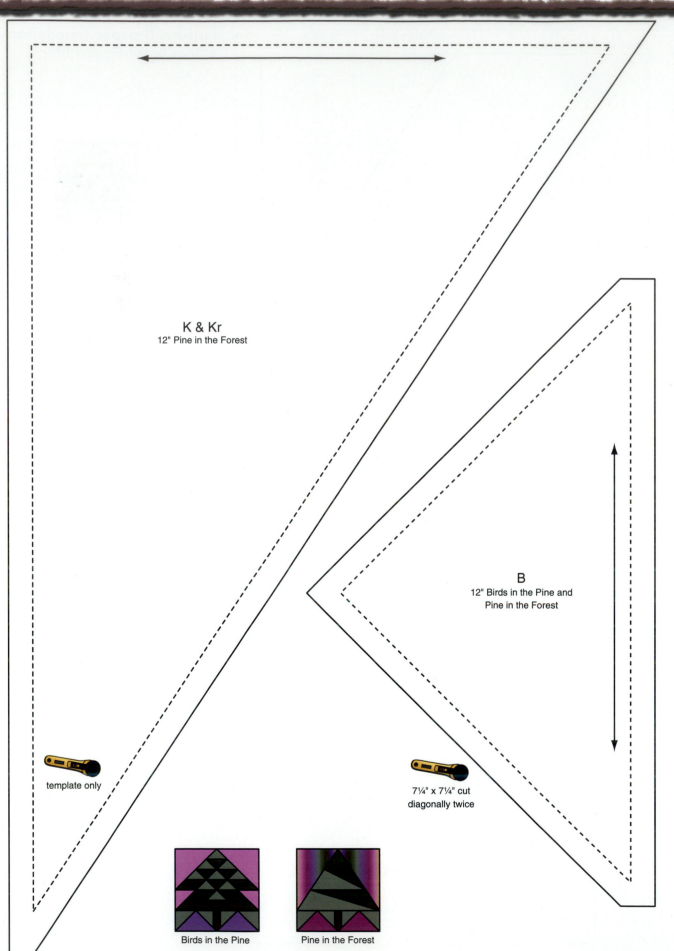

K & Kr
12" Pine in the Forest

B
12" Birds in the Pine and
Pine in the Forest

template only

7¼" x 7¼" cut
diagonally twice

Birds in the Pine

Pine in the Forest

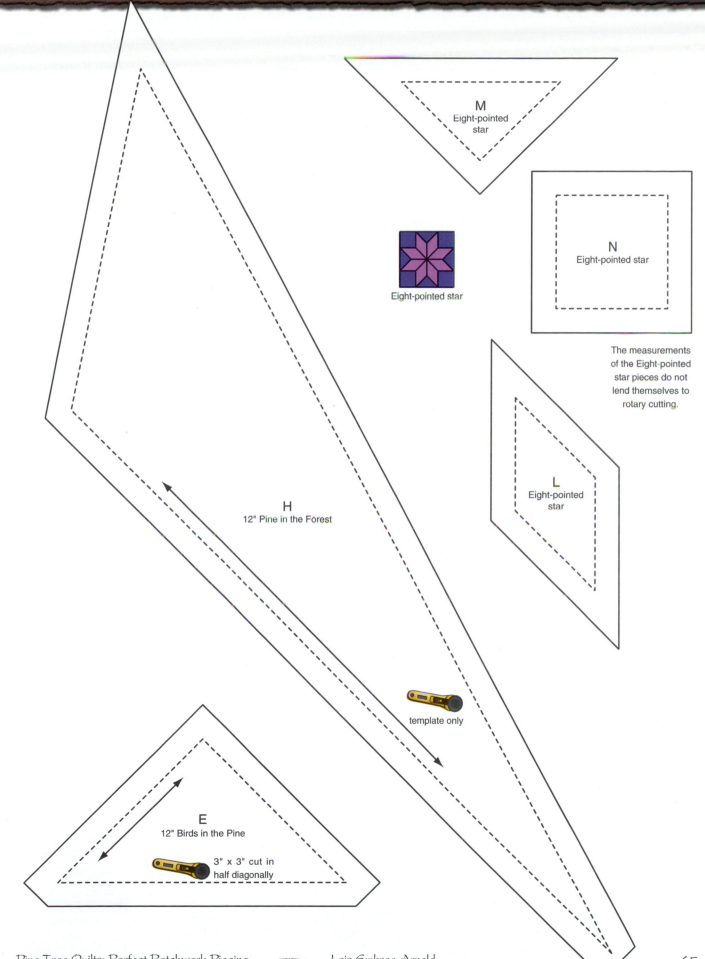

M
Eight-pointed star

Eight-pointed star

N
Eight-pointed star

The measurements of the Eight-pointed star pieces do not lend themselves to rotary cutting.

L
Eight-pointed star

H
12" Pine in the Forest

template only

E
12" Birds in the Pine

3" x 3" cut in half diagonally

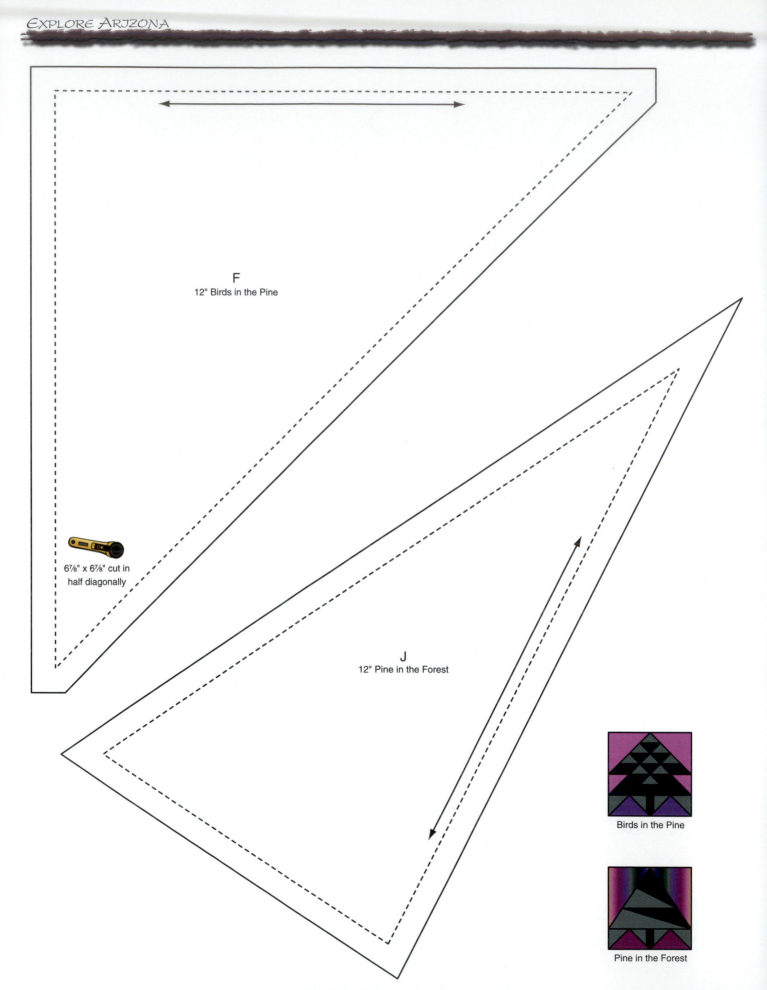

F
12" Birds in the Pine

6⅞" x 6⅞" cut in half diagonally

J
12" Pine in the Forest

Birds in the Pine

Pine in the Forest

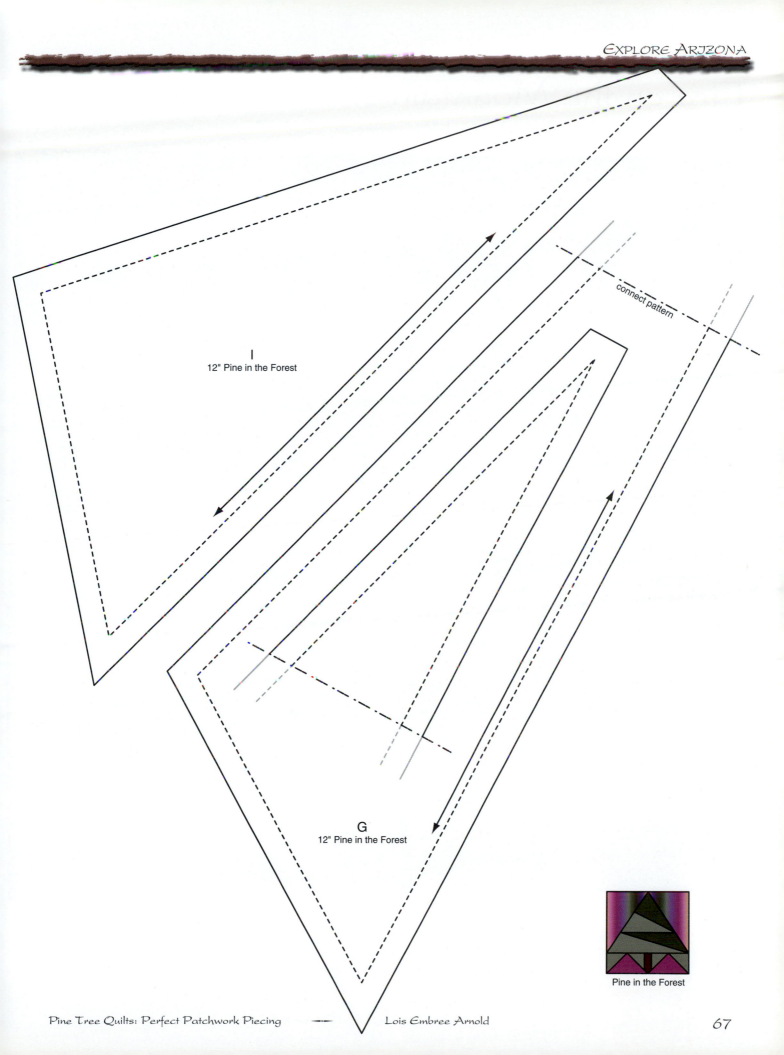

I
12" Pine in the Forest

connect pattern

G
12" Pine in the Forest

Pine in the Forest

Fire on the Mountain

Quilt: 51½" x 51½"
Finished blocks: 12" x 12"
4 whole blocks   4 half blocks

FIRE ON THE MOUNTAIN (51" x 51") by the author.
This quilt was created to honor the many trees lost to forest fires each year, especially in the Southwestern United States. The black triangles represent the skeletons of the trees, and the brightly colored "fire" triangles illuminate them.

FABRIC REQUIREMENTS AND CUTTING

Fabrics*	Yards	Pieces
†Fire prints:		
trees	¼ ea. color	240 F, 32 H
sashing	⅓	16 K
Brown 1	¼	4 B, 48 D
Brown 2	⅛	4 A, 8 F
Background:	3½	4A, 4 C, 4 Cr, 8 D, 24 E, 240 F, 13 G, 32 H, 20 I, 4 J, 32 K
border		4 strips 5" x 52½"
binding		6 strips 2½" x fabric width
Backing	3¼	2 panels 28" x 55"
Batting	—	55" x 55"

*Yardage based on 42"-wide fabric.

†Red, orange, yellow–at least 7 colors

PINE TREE BLOCK

1. Sew a background F triangle and a fire-print F triangle together to make a half-square unit. Make 240 half-square units.

2. Assemble the block, following the steps in Figure 4–11. Make four blocks.

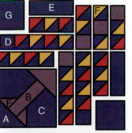

Figure 4–11.
Block assembly:
(a) Patch placement.

(b) Sew the patches and units into rows and the rows into sections.

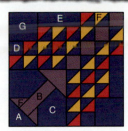

(c) Join sections to complete the block.

HALF BLOCK

3. Sew two H triangles together to make the unit shown in Figure 4–12. Make 32 units.

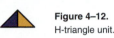

Figure 4–12.
H-triangle unit.

4. Follow Figure 4–13 to make eight half blocks.

 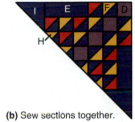

Figure 4–13.
Half block assembly. **(a)** Sew patches and units into rows, and rows into sections.

(b) Sew sections together.

SASHING

5. Sew a print K strip (1½" by width of fabric) between two black K strips. Cut the sewn strips into 12½" lengths (Figure 4–14). Make 16 sashing units 3½" x 12½".

Figure 4–14.
Making sashing units.

QUILT ASSEMBLY

6. Assemble blocks, half blocks, sashes, and G, I, and J setting pieces in diagonal rows, following Figure 4–15.

7. Sew the border strips to the quilt top and miter the corners as described on pages 36–38.

8. Layer and baste the backing, batting, and quilt top. Quilt as desired. In the quilt pictured on page 68, flame shapes of various sizes were machine quilted in variegated rayon thread across the surface and in the border.

9. Bind the quilt and attach a label.

Figure 4–15.
Quilt assembly.

FIRE ON THE MOUNTAIN detail.

ROTARY-CUT C/CR PATCHES

You can make a template from the pattern on the facing page, or you can use the following rotary cutting method to make these patches:

For each block, cut two rectangles 3½" x 4¾". Place them wrong sides together. Use pencil or chalk to mark a dot 1⅜" down from the top on the left side and 2¼" down from the top on the right side of the rectangle.

Align the 45-degree line on your ruler along the right side of the rectangle, with the edge of the ruler on the dot marked at 1⅜", and cut off the left triangle. Align the 45-degree line along the left side of the rectangle, with the edge of the ruler on the dot marked at 2¼", and cut off the right triangle. You will have two mirror-image house-shaped pieces.

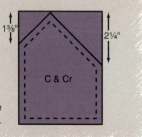

For rotary-cut C and Cr patches, use the 45-degree line on your ruler to cut the corners from the rectangles.

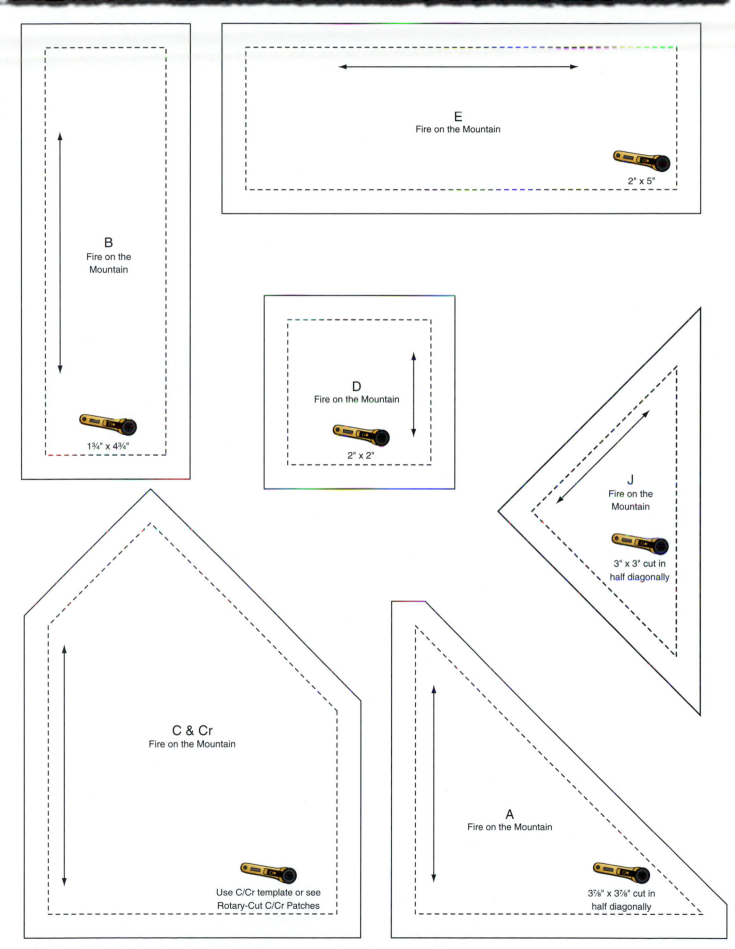

B
Fire on the
Mountain

1¾" x 4¾"

E
Fire on the Mountain

2" x 5"

D
Fire on the Mountain

2" x 2"

J
Fire on the
Mountain

3" x 3" cut in
half diagonally

C & Cr
Fire on the Mountain

Use C/Cr template or see
Rotary-Cut C/Cr Patches

A
Fire on the Mountain

3⅞" x 3⅞" cut in
half diagonally

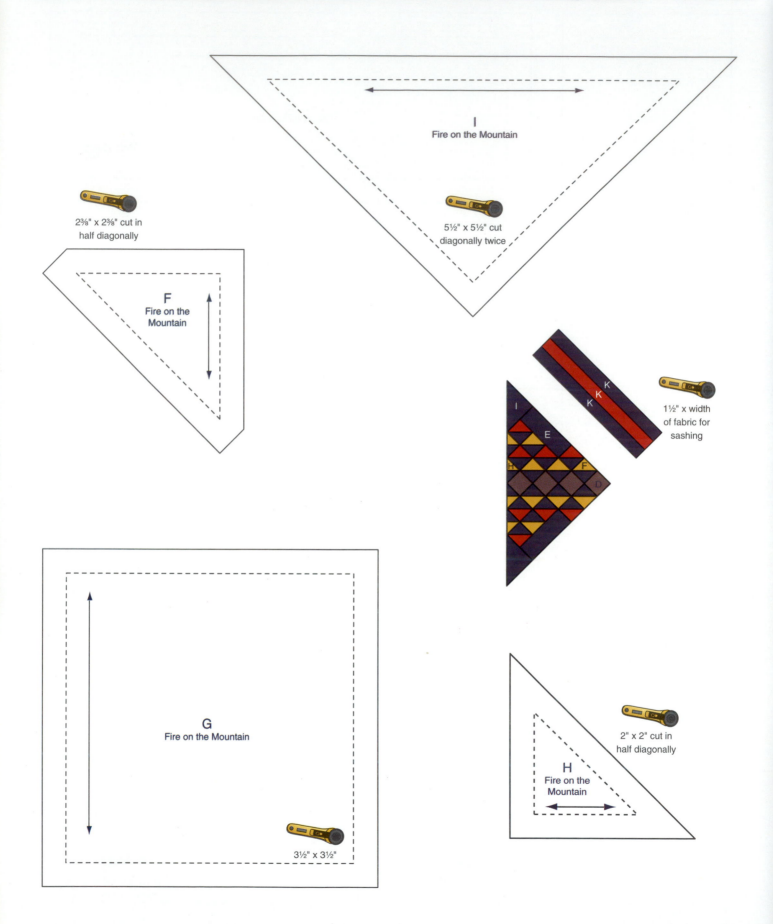

I
Fire on the Mountain

5½" x 5½" cut
diagonally twice

2⅜" x 2⅜" cut in
half diagonally

F
Fire on the
Mountain

1½" x width
of fabric for
sashing

G
Fire on the Mountain

3½" x 3½"

2" x 2" cut in
half diagonally

H
Fire on the
Mountain

Happy Trees

HAPPY TREES (62" x 59") by Linda Yantis.
This quilt is a reproduction of an antique that never fails to make people smile.
The original is made in bright colors from the 1940s. Linda was asked to make this
appliquéd quilt a happy one like the antique, so she chose her favorite reproduction 1930s fabrics.

FABRIC REQUIREMENTS AND CUTTING

Fabrics*	Yards	Pieces
White:	3¼	20 rectangles 9½" x 12½"
border 2		2 strips 5½" x 61½"
		2 strips 5½" x 54½"
Tree prints	20 fat ⅛'s	20 B, 20 C, 20 D, 20 E, 20 F
Brown: trunks	⅛	20 A
Print:	1⅝	
border 1		4 strips 2½" x 51"
binding		7 strips 2½" x 42"
Backing	3¾	2 panels 34" x 63"
Batting	—	63" x 66"

*Yardage based on 42"-wide fabric.

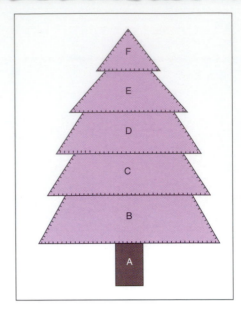

(b) Sew around each piece with the buttonhole stitch.

APPLIQUÉD TREES

1. Prepare the background rectangles for appliqué by folding them in half horizontally and vertically to find the centers. Press in the folds.

2. Center the trunk (patch A) approximately ½" up from the bottom edge of the background rectangle. Use needle-turn appliqué (page 33) on sides and bottom of trunk.

3. Center bottom of tree (patch B) on block above the trunk with approximately ½" overlapping trunk. When the patch B ¼" seam allowance is turned under, it should cover the raw edge of the trunk.

4. Continue in the same manner with remaining tree pieces C–F.

5. After all pieces have been appliquéd, use matching or contrasting perle cotton or two to three strands of embroidery floss to sew a buttonhole stitch around each piece (Figure 4–16). Make 20 blocks.

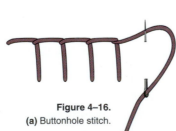

Figure 4–16.
(a) Buttonhole stitch.

6. Following the photo of the quilt, stitch four rows of five blocks each.

BORDERS AND FINISHING

7. Sew a print border strip to each side of the quilt and trim the ends even with the quilt edge. Sew border strips to the top and bottom; trim.

8. Sew the background borders to the quilt as you did for the first border.

9. Follow general directions on page 38 to layer the top, batting, and backing. Baste and quilt as desired. An all-over fan design was quilted over the entire surface of the quilt pictured on page 73.

10. Bind the quilt as described on pages 38–40.

HAPPY TREES detail.

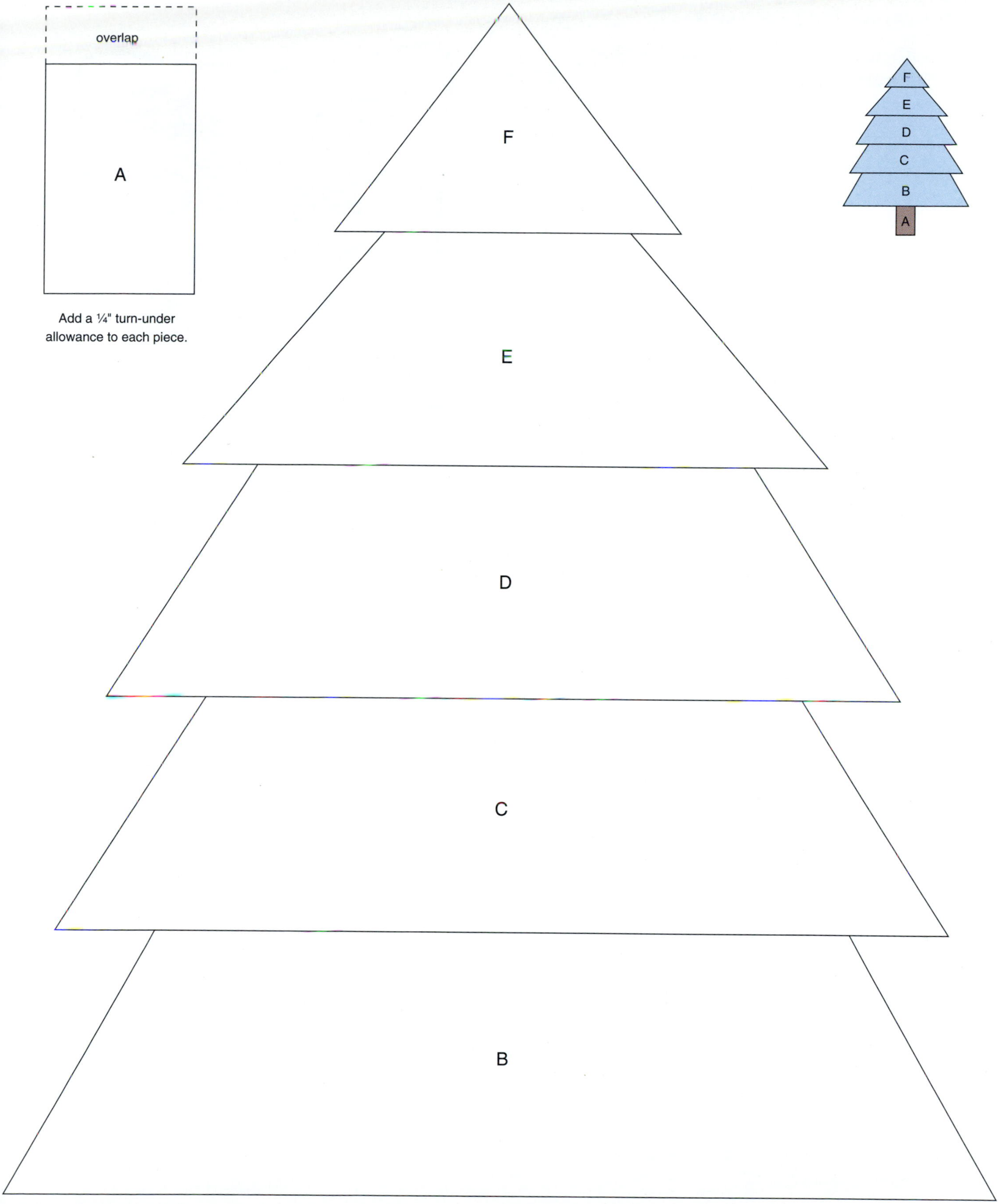

overlap

A

Add a ¼" turn-under allowance to each piece.

F

E

D

C

B

HAWAIIAN PINES PILLOW

Fabric Requirements and Cutting

Fabrics*	Yards	Pieces
White:	⅝	1 square 18" x 18"
lapped back		2 rectangles 16½" x 11½"
Green	⅝	1 square 18" x 18"
Pillow-top backing	⅝	1 square 20" x 20"
Cording	2	
Freezer paper	—	1 square 16" x 16"
Batting	—	1 square 19" x 19"
Pillow form	—	16" x 16"

*Yardage based on 42"-wide fabric.

HAWAIIAN PINES by the author.

Here is another happy little tree. On the Island of Maui, Hawaii, there are trees with almost ruffled needles, known as Cook Island or Norfolk pines. They were first planted in the 1880s. While these Hawaiian trees belong to a different species, they look similar to pines. This Hawaiian-style appliqué was designed in their honor. Using a simple shape and paper-folding technique, you can make your own version, which can be as intricate or simple as you like.

Pillow Construction

1. Fold the background fabric in half horizontally, vertically, and diagonally. Center the design on the background by using the creases in the fabric to guide the placement of the trees so the tips point toward the corners of the square.

2. Secure the design to the background with pins or use a mechanical pencil to draw around the freezer-paper design. Remove the freezer paper and baste about ¼" inside the edges of the design. Using an invisible stitch, appliqué the trees to the background.

3. Layer the backing fabric, batting, and pillow top; baste. Echo quilt in rows about ¼" apart around the design until a 16" x 16" area has been covered. Using rotary-cutting tools, trim the layers to 16½" x 16½", making sure the design remains centered.

4. For the lapped pillow back, hem one long edge of each rectangle by pressing under ¼". Press under another ¼" on the same edges and sew in place (Figure 4–17).

5. Cut green bias strips wide enough to cover the cording and leave a generous seam allowance. Sew the strips together, end to end, with a diagonal seam. Wrap the fabric, right side out, around the cording. Use either a zipper foot or a special cording foot to stitch as close as possible to the cord. Trim the seam allowance to ¼".

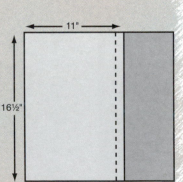

Figure 4–17.
Lapped pillow back. Hem one long edge of each piece.

6. Clip the cording seam allowance to obtain a smooth corner. Sew the cording to the pillow top, matching the cut edges and curving the corners slightly, if desired.

7. Place the two halves that form the lapped back, right sides together, on the pillow front. Sew, following the previous row of stitching for the cording.

8. Clip the corners, turn the pillow right side out, and slip in the pillow form.

How to Transfer Pattern

1. Fold the 16" square of freezer paper in half horizontally. Fold in half again vertically, forming an 8" square. There are four layers of paper at this point. Make two diagonal folds, bringing the top two layers to the horizontal fold to form a triangle. Fold the bottom two layers to the back to complete the triangle shape as shown in Figure 4–18. (Folding all four layers to the front will not give an accurate crease because of the thickness of the paper.)

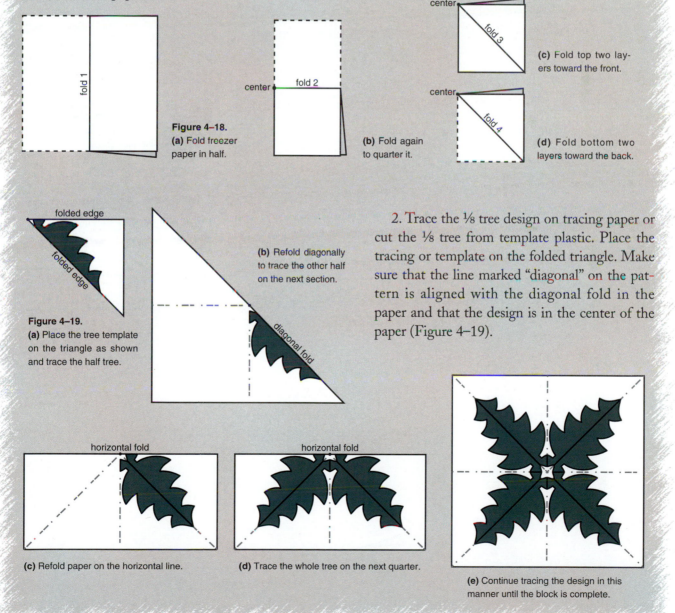

Figure 4–18.
(a) Fold freezer paper in half.
(b) Fold again to quarter it.
(c) Fold top two layers toward the front.
(d) Fold bottom two layers toward the back.

2. Trace the ⅛ tree design on tracing paper or cut the ⅛ tree from template plastic. Place the tracing or template on the folded triangle. Make sure that the line marked "diagonal" on the pattern is aligned with the diagonal fold in the paper and that the design is in the center of the paper (Figure 4–19).

Figure 4–19.
(a) Place the tree template on the triangle as shown and trace the half tree.
(b) Refold diagonally to trace the other half on the next section.
(c) Refold paper on the horizontal line.
(d) Trace the whole tree on the next quarter.
(e) Continue tracing the design in this manner until the block is complete.

3. Go over the lines with a permanent marker so the design can be easily seen. To transfer the rest of the design, unfold the paper and refold along the diagonal. Using a light box, retrace the 1/8 design to complete the tree shape. You now have one fourth of the design. Refold the paper in half on the horizontal line and trace the full tree shape. At this point, you will have traced half the design. Refold the paper in half vertically and retrace to complete the design.

4. Unfold the paper to cut the completed tree design with scissors. Cutting only one layer is much more accurate than trying to cut through all the layers.

5. Fold the 16" square of green fabric in half horizontally. Then fold vertically and diagonally, creasing each fold.

6. Open the fabric and center the completed paper tree design on the fabric. Iron the freezer paper to the fabric. Then cut around the design, leaving a seam allowance of between 1/8" and 1/4" beyond the edges of the paper. The narrower seam allowance is easier to appliqué.

diagonal fold

center

Quilt: 18" x 18"
Finished blocks:
4 Pine Trees 4" x 4"
4 Compass Stars 0" x 0"

If You Go Into the Woods Today, Don't Forget Your Compass

IF YOU GO INTO THE WOODS TODAY, DON'T FORGET YOUR COMPASS (18" x 18") by the author.
That's wonderful advice for anyone who plans to explore a forest! This tiny quilt seemed to call for a very long name.

FABRIC REQUIREMENTS AND CUTTING

Fabrics*	Yards	Pieces
Green:	scraps	
trees, star points		8 E, 8 F, 8 G, 8 I, 16 K
border triangles	⅓	4 strips 2½" x 42"
Brown: trunks	scraps	4 A
Gold: star centers	scrap	4 J
Red:	¼	
star points		16 L
border		4 strips 1¼" x 12½"
White:	⅞	8 B, 4 C, 12 D, 12 Dr,
		4 H, 4 Hr, 32 M
star background		4 squares 4" x 4"
corner triangles		2 squares 8" x 8"
border		2 strips 2½" x 42"
Backing	¾	1 panel 22" x 22"
Binding	¼	3 strips 1¾" x 42"
Batting	—	22" x 22"

*Yardage based on 42"-wide fabric.

PINE TREES

1. To assemble the trunk unit, sew a B triangle to each side of the trunk (Figure 4–20).

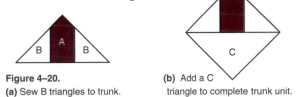

Figure 4–20.
(a) Sew B triangles to trunk.
(b) Add a C triangle to complete trunk unit.

2. Sew the tree branches as shown in Figure 4–21 to make half-blocks. Join the halves with a diagonal seam, stopping and backstitching ¼" away from the edge.

3. To add the trunk unit, sew one side of the unit to the lower edge of the branch unit, sewing from edge to edge. Fold the branch unit diagonally to expose the final seam. Sew from the outside edge toward the center, stopping at the cross seam. Make four blocks.

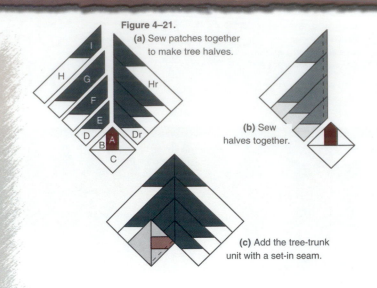

Figure 4–21.
(a) Sew patches together to make tree halves.
(b) Sew halves together.
(c) Add the tree-trunk unit with a set-in seam.

4. Join the four tree blocks (Figure 4–22). Cut the 8" white squares in half diagonally to form the corner triangles. Center two of the triangles on opposite sides of the quilt and sew. Repeat with the other two triangles. Square and trim the quilt to 12½". The trees will "float" in the background when the border is added.

5. Paper piece each border strip in two sections (Figure 4–23). Make four borders strips.

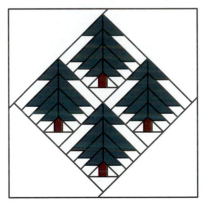

Figure 4–22.
Sew the four tree blocks together and add corner triangles.

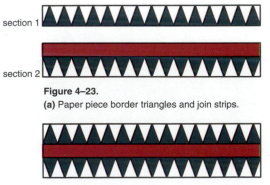

section 1

section 2

Figure 4–23.
(a) Paper piece border triangles and join strips.
(b) Completed border strip.

PAPER-PIECED BORDER

To make paper piecing the borders easier and keep the border on the straight of grain, you can precut the triangles from the 2½" green border strips. On a rotary-cutting mat, lay the 2½" strips, wrong side up, below and parallel to the paper foundation. Lay a ruler along one triangle side and cut the fabric strip with a rotary cutter. Align the ruler with the other side of the triangle to make the second cut (refer to Figure 3–10, page 35). These triangles need to be approximately 1⅝" wide at the lower edge for the seam allowances.

COMPASS STAR

6. Piece the Compass Star in four sections, as shown in Figure 4–24. Make 16 sections.

7. Join four sections to form a star. Hand appliqué the gold circle (J) to the center. Hand appliqué the Compass Star to a 4" background square, centering it so the red points are pointing north, east, south, and west. Square and trim block to measure 3½". Make four blocks.

QUILT ASSEMBLY

8. Sew a pieced border on two opposite sides of the quilt. Join one Compass Star block to each end of the two remaining borders and sew the borders to the top and bottom (Figure 4–25).

9. Layer the top, batting, and backing, and baste. Quilt as desired. The author's quilt was quilted in the ditch around the shapes in the tree blocks, borders, and compass blocks. The compass design was enlarged and half of it was used in the setting triangles. A second row of compass points was added, echoing the design. Bind the raw edges, following directions on pages 38–40.

Figure 4–24.
(a) Piece K, L, and M patches to make sections.

(b) Join four sections to make the star and appliqué a J circle to the center.

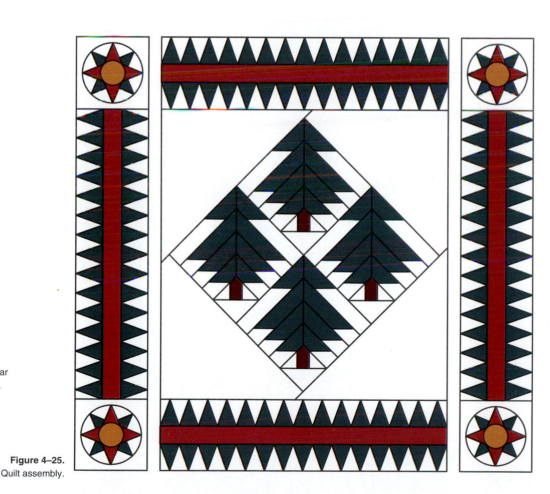

Figure 4–25.
Quilt assembly.

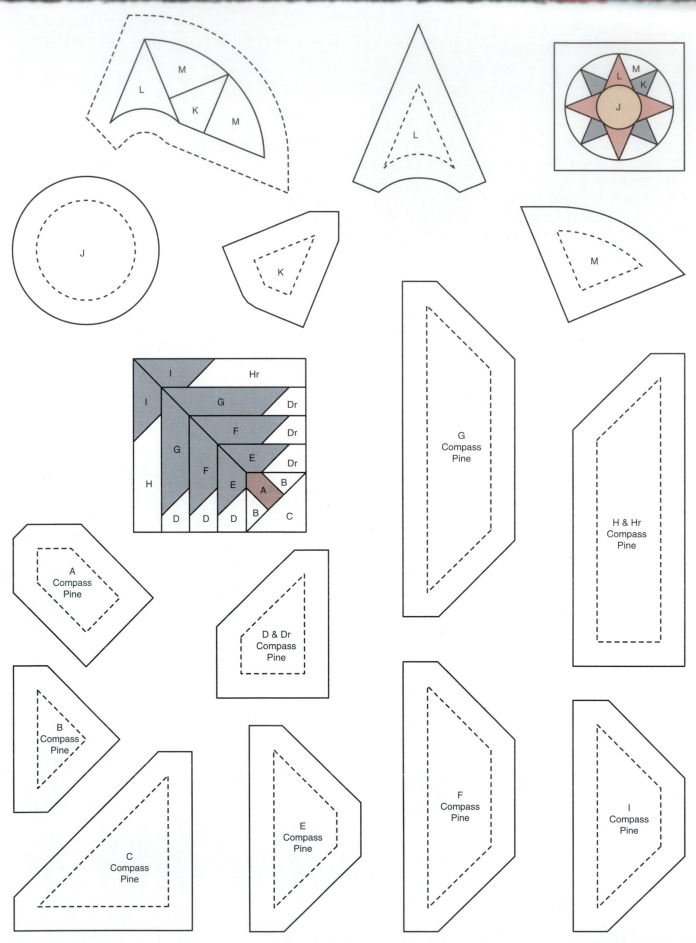

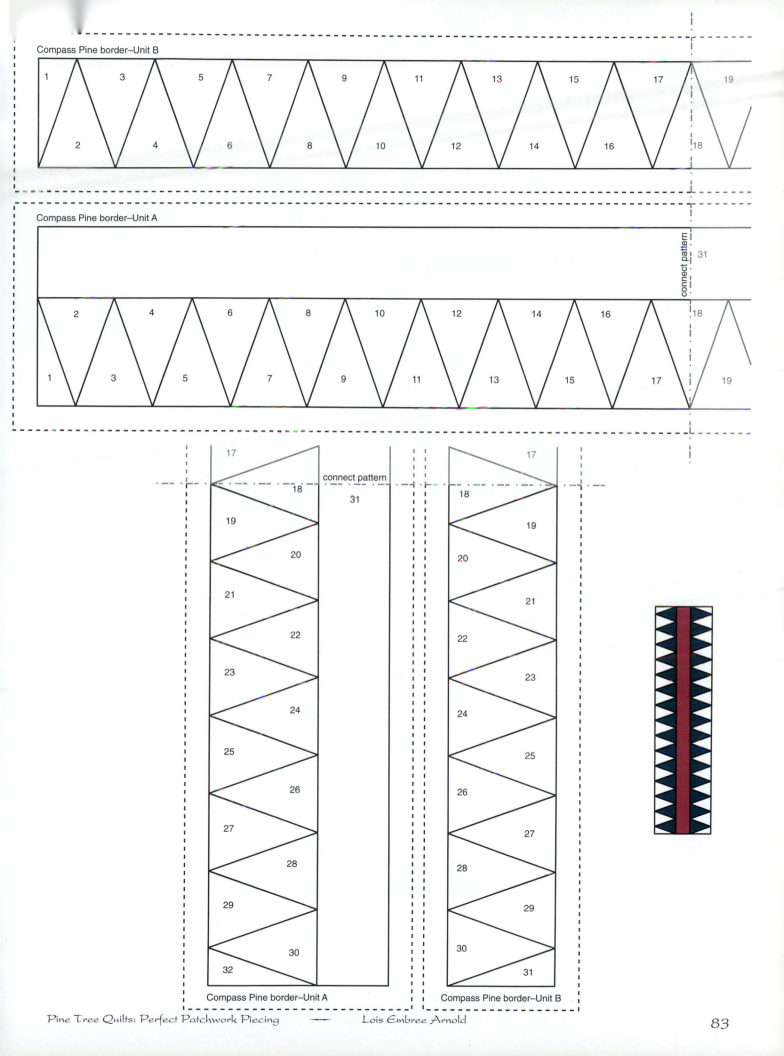

Compass Pine border—Unit B

Compass Pine border—Unit A

connect pattern

17 18 19 20 21 22 23 24 25 26 27 28 29 30 32

Compass Pine border—Unit A

17 18 19 20 21 22 23 24 25 26 27 28 29 30 31

Compass Pine border—Unit B

Log Cabin Pines

Quilt: 27" x 27"
Finished block: 6" x 6"

LOG CABIN PINES (27" x 27") pieced by Carol Deloney and machine quilted by Donna Reed.
These handsome Pine Tree blocks are made Log Cabin-style. Instructions are provided for
traditional piecing as well as paper-foundation piecing.

FABRIC REQUIREMENTS AND CUTTING

Fabrics*	Yards	Pieces
Tree branches	⅝	12 B, 12 D
binding		3 strips 1¾" x 42"
Trunk	scrap	4 F
Background:	½	8 A, 8 C, 8 E, 4 G
corner triangles		2 squares 11" x 11"
Accent:	¼	
border 1		2 strips 1¼" x 14½"
		2 strips 1¼" x 16"
border 2		2 strips 1½" x 21½"
		2 strips 1½" x 23½"
Pieced border:		
light print	⅜	144 A
dark print	⅜	144 A
Backing	⅞	1 panel 30" x 30"
Batting	—	28" x 28"

*Yardage based on 42"-wide fabric.

LOG CABIN PINE

1. Referring to the block assembly diagram, (Figure 4–26), make four of each branch unit A/B, B/C, A/D, and C/D.

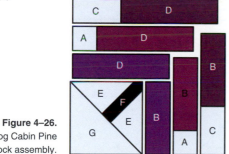

Figure 4–26.
Log Cabin Pine
block assembly.

2. At this point, you may choose to continue by paper piecing the four blocks for greater accuracy or skip to Step 3.

For paper piecing, make four copies of the block pattern on page 86 by tracing or photo copying. Paper piece the blocks, following the directions on page 35.

3. To make a trunk unit using regular piecing, sew an E patch to each side of the trunk (F), aligning the bottoms of the pieces. If you rotary cut F as a rectangle, use a square ruler to trim the trunk even with the triangles (Figure 4–27). Add the G triangle to complete the unit. Make four trunk units.

Figure 4–27.
Use a square ruler to trim the trunk.

4. Sew the trunk and branch units together to finish the block. Make four blocks.

QUILT ASSEMBLY

5. Join the blocks in pairs, then join the pairs to form a square (see quilt assembly, Figure 4–28).

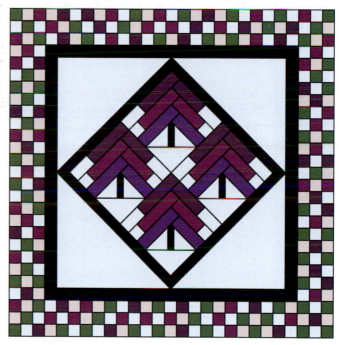

Figure 4–28.
Quilt assembly.

6. Sew the 1¼" x 14½" border-1 strips to opposite sides of the square. Trim the ends even with the quilt. Sew the two 1¼" x 16" border strips to the remaining sides and trim.

7. Cut the 11" background squares in half diagonally to make the corner triangles. Center a corner triangle on the square, right sides together, and sew the

seam. Sew a second triangle to the opposite side. Repeat with the remaining two triangles. Trim the square to measure 19½".

8. For border 2, sew the two 1½" x 21½" strips to the top and bottom of the quilt. Trim even with the quilt. Sew the 1½" x 23½" strips to the sides and trim.

9. To construct border 3, make 32 nine-patch units, 16 with five dark squares and 16 with five light squares (Figure 4–29). Join the nine-patches, alternating light and dark, in two rows of seven and two rows of nine. Sew the shorter rows to the top and bottom of the quilt, then sew the longer rows to the sides to finish the border.

10. Layer quilt top, batting and back. Baste and quilt as desired. The photographed quilt was free-motion quilted in tree shapes. Free-hand pine branches and needles were quilted with contrasting thread in the setting triangles. Meandering quilting was used in the background of the trees and in the borders. The pieced border was quilted in a cross-hatched grid. Bind the edges, following the directions on pages 38–40.

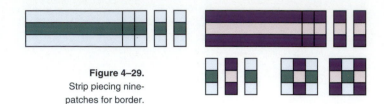

Figure 4–29.
Strip piecing nine-patches for border.

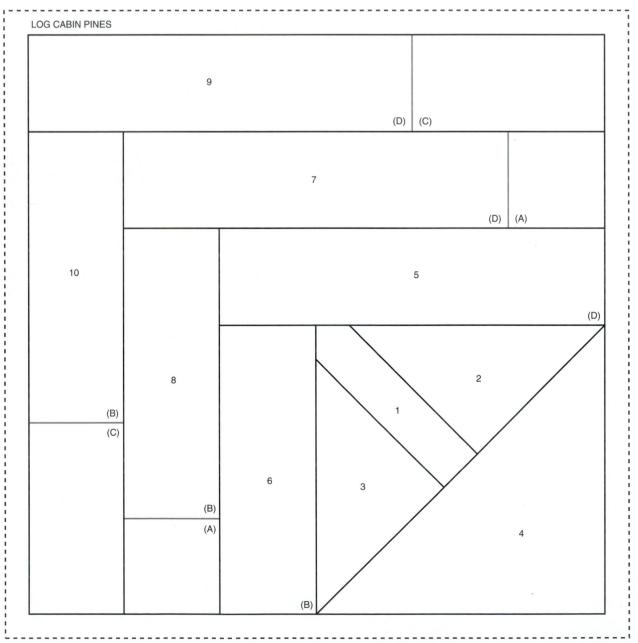

Log Cabin Pines can be paper foundation pieced by using the full-sized pattern on page 86, or pieced the traditional way with the patch patterns on this page.

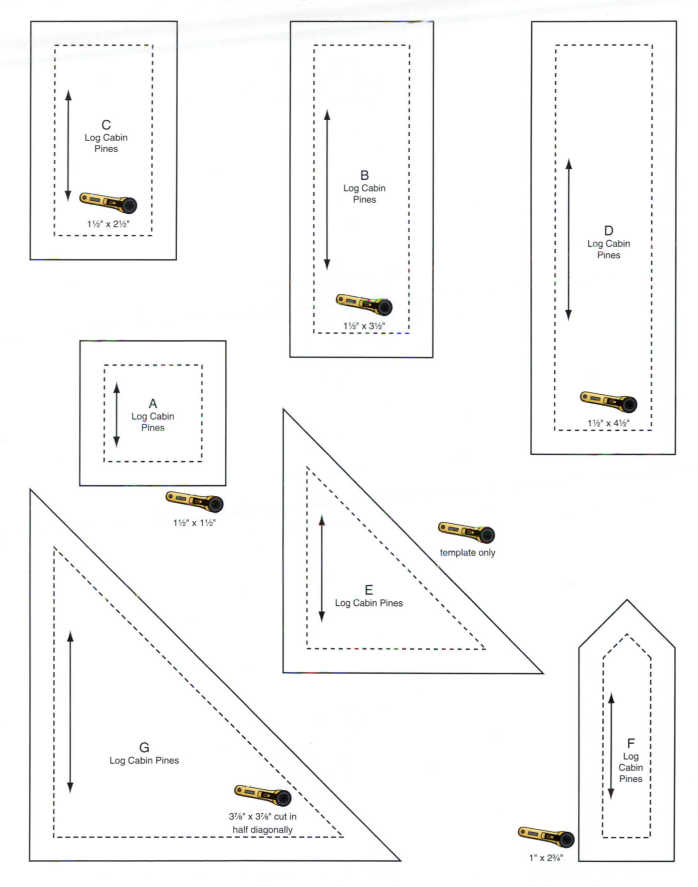

C
Log Cabin Pines

1½" x 2½"

B
Log Cabin Pines

1½" x 3½"

D
Log Cabin Pines

1½" x 4½"

A
Log Cabin Pines

1½" x 1½"

E
Log Cabin Pines

template only

G
Log Cabin Pines

3⅞" x 3⅞" cut in half diagonally

F
Log Cabin Pines

1" x 2¾"

Pine Burr
Table
Runner

Table runner: 18" x 60½"
Finished block: 10" x 10"

PINE BURR table runner (17" x 57") by the author.
Make your table look festive any time with this Pine Burr table runner. You can make it in a hurry by
rotary cutting and machine piecing the patches, or take your time by cutting templates and hand piecing.

FABRIC REQUIREMENTS AND CUTTING

Fabric*	Yards	Pieces
Dark blue	¼	4 A
Light blue print	¼	16 B
Light blue	¼	16 C
Medium blue print	¼	112 D
Yellow:	1⅞	144 D
side triangles		2 squares 15½" x 15½"
corner triangles		2 squares 8" x 8"
borders		5 strips 2½" x 42"
binding		5 strips 1¾" x 42"
Backing	1	2 panels 21" x 33"
Batting	—	21" x 65½"

*Yardage based on 42"-wide fabric.

PINE BURR

1. Cut the patches listed in the Fabric Requirements and Cutting chart, as follows: Make a template for triangle B. Cut two 4" strips across the width of the fabric. Use the template to cut the triangles from the strips.

2. Cut the C and D squares in half diagonally to make the half-square triangles. Sew a blue and a yellow D triangle together to make a half-square unit. Make 112 units.

3. Following the block assembly diagram (Figure 4–30), sew seven half-square units and two yellow D patches to a C triangle to make a corner unit. Make 16 corner units.

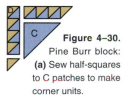

Figure 4–30.
Pine Burr block:
(a) Sew half-squares to C patches to make corner units.

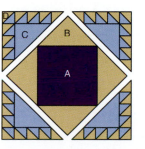

(b) Add corner units to center square to complete block.

4. Sew one A and four B patches together to make the center square-within-a-square unit. Make four units.

5. Add four corner units to each square-within-a-square unit to complete the blocks. The blocks should measure 10½" x 10½", including seam allowances.

QUILT ASSEMBLY

6. Cut the 15½" yellow squares twice diagonally to make six side triangles. There will be two extra triangles. Cut the 8" yellow squares once diagonally for the corner triangles.

7. Sew the blocks and side triangles together in diagonal rows (Figure 4–31). Sew the rows together. Add the corner triangles.

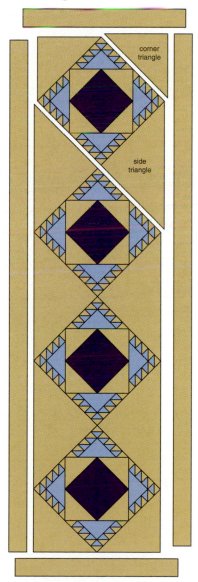

corner triangle

side triangle

Figure 4–31.
Quilt assembly.

8. For the borders, piece the yellow 2½" strips end to end, with diagonal seams, to create the lengths needed.

9. Center and sew the borders to the quilt, stopping and starting ¼" in from the edge at the corners. Miter the corners, following the directions on page 38.

10. Layer the backing, batting, and quilt top. Baste and quilt as desired. Each blue square was quilted with a simple flower and four leaves. Feathers of the appropriate size were quilted in the light blue triangles and in the side and corner triangles. Free-motion quilting in a stippled pattern was used in all the open areas. Bind the quilted runner with the yellow 1¾" strips.

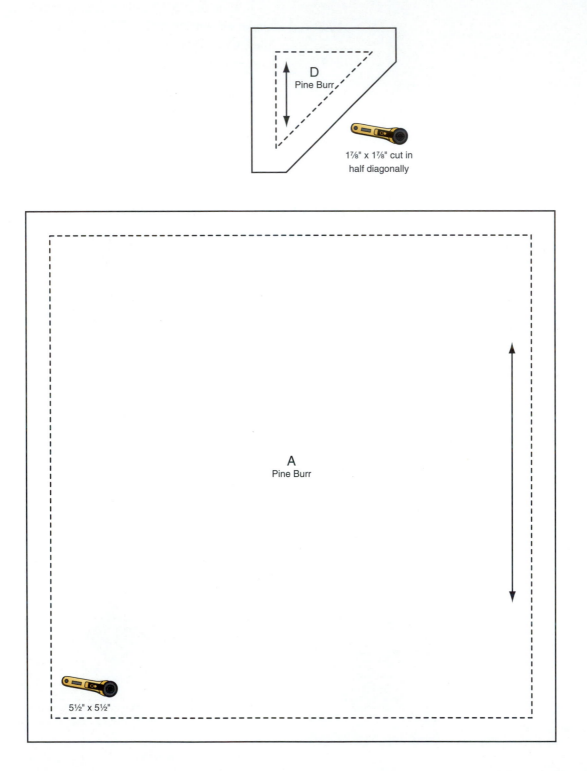

D
Pine Burr

1⅞" x 1⅞" cut in
half diagonally

A
Pine Burr

5½" x 5½"

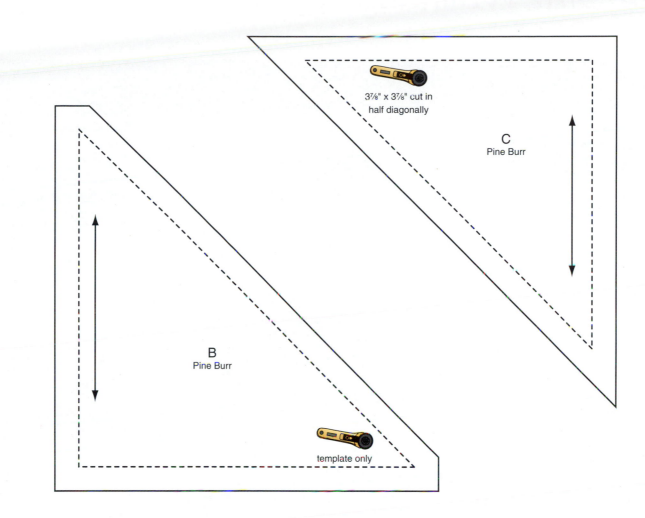

3⅞" x 3⅞" cut in
half diagonally

C
Pine Burr

B
Pine Burr

template only

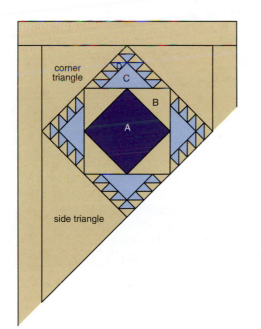

corner
triangle

D
C
B
A

side triangle

Corner
Triangles

8" x 8"
cut in half diagonally

Side
Triangles

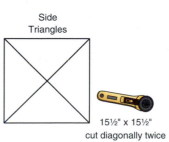

15½" x 15½"
cut diagonally twice

Pine Star Wallhanging

Quilt: 48" x 48"
8 Finished blocks: 10" x 10"

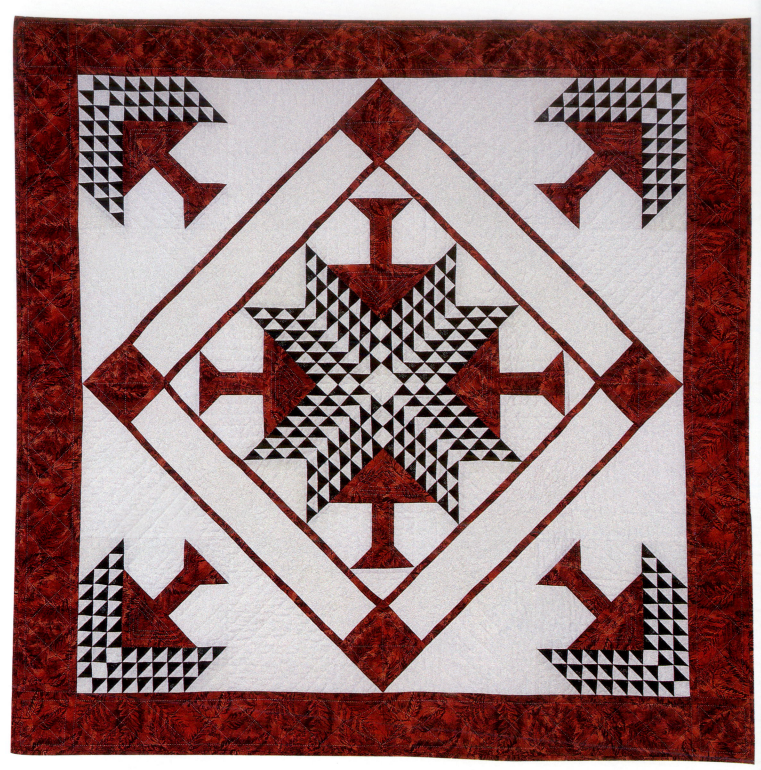

PINE STAR (48" x 48") by the author.
Originally, this quilt was to be a full-sized bed quilt. It almost didn't get made at all when the rust fabric used in the tree trunks bled. The trunk units were replaced and enough blocks were salvaged to make the wall quilt. The quilting design was adapted from antique oak pressed-back chairs.

FABRIC REQUIREMENTS AND CUTTING

Fabrics*	Yards	Pieces
Dark green	⅝	336 E
Rust:	2	16 B, 8 C, 8 D
borders 1 and 3		8 strips 1" x 20½"
corner squares		4 squares 4½" x 4½"
border 4		4 strips 4½" x 51"
binding		5 strips 1¾" x 42"
White	1¾	16 A, 288 E,
		24 F, 24 G
side triangles		4 squares 11" x 11"
border 2		4 strips 3½" x 20½"
Backing	3	2 panels 26" x 51"

*Yardage based on 42"-wide fabric.

BLOCK ASSEMBLY

1. Divide the house-shaped A patches into two piles. Sew B triangles on the right sides of the A patches in one pile and on the left sides in the second pile.

2. Join the A/B units to the C trunks (Figure 4–32a).

3. Add D triangles to the tops of the units and G triangles to the bottoms to complete the trunk units.

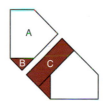

Figure 4–32.
Block assembly: **(a)** Join the A/B units to the C trunks.

(b) Add D and G patches to complete trunk unit.

4. Sew the dark green and white E triangles together to make half-square units. Join the units into sections as shown in Figure 4–32c.

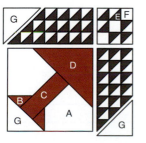

(c) Join half-square units in sections.

5. Sew the sections and trunk units together and attach the G triangles at the corners to complete the block. Make eight blocks.

6. Sew one background 3½" x 20½" strip between two rust 1" x 20½" strips to form a border unit (Figure 4–33). Make 4 units.

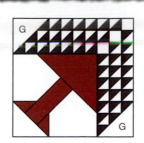

(d) Join the sections and the G triangles to complete the blocks.

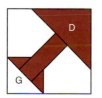

Figure 4–33.
Borders: **(a)** Sew one light and two dark strips together to make a border unit.

(b) Add squares to two of the border units.

7. Sew four tree blocks together, with branches touching, to form the medallion center.

8. Sew two border units to opposite sides of the medallion center. Sew 4½" corner squares to each end of the two remaining border units. Sew the units to the other two sides (Figure 4–34 on the following page).

9. Cut the 11" squares in half diagonally to make the side triangles. Referring to the quilt assembly diagram, sew two side triangles to each remaining tree block. Sew these corner units to the medallion center.

10. Add the border strips to each side of the wall quilt and miter the corners (page 38).

11. Layer the top, batting, and backing. Baste and quilt as desired. The author quilted the half-square unit diagonals and continued the lines into the background. The trunks were quilted ¼" from the seams, and triangles D and G were echo quilted, ¼" apart. The quilting pattern, page 94, was used in Border 2, and stippling fills the rest of the space. The corner squares were outlined, and an X was quilted corner to corner. The outside border has squares on point. Bind the raw edges, following basic directions on pages 38–40.

Figure 4–34.
Quilt assembly.

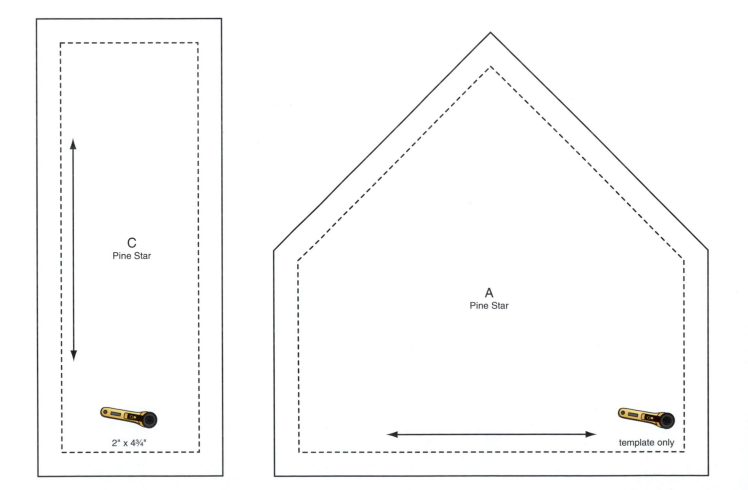

C
Pine Star

2" x 4¾"

A
Pine Star

template only

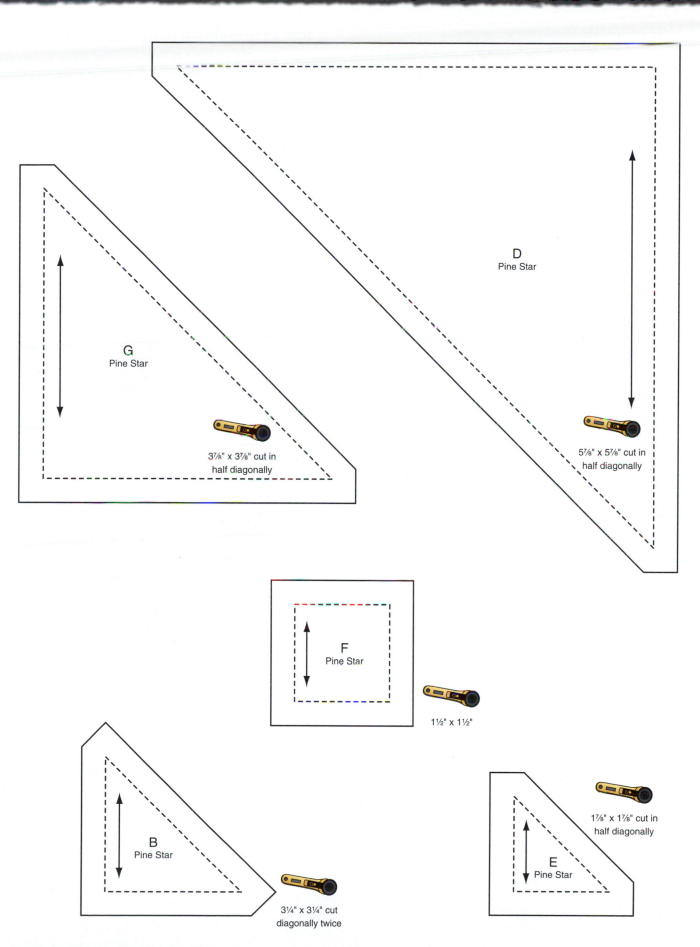

D
Pine Star

G
Pine Star

3⅞" x 3⅞" cut in
half diagonally

5⅞" x 5⅞" cut in
half diagonally

F
Pine Star

1½" x 1½"

1⅞" x 1⅞" cut in
half diagonally

B
Pine Star

E
Pine Star

3¼" x 3¼" cut
diagonally twice

PINE STAR Quilting pattern for Border 2.

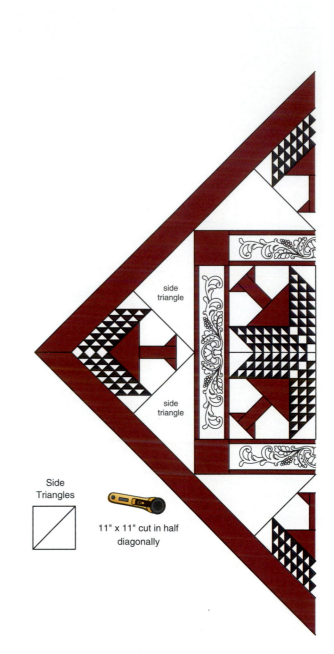

side triangle

side triangle

Side Triangles

11" x 11" cut in half diagonally

Redwood Forest

REDWOOD FOREST (90" x 90") by the author.
Viewing the Redwood Forest for the first time is an experience one cannot forget.
The age and enormity of these trees were the inspiration for this quilt.

FABRIC REQUIREMENTS AND CUTTING

Fabrics*	Yards	Pieces
Red:	5	16 A, 16 B, 9 D, 192 E, 768 F, 12 H, 4 I, 128 J
border		10 strips 2½" x 42"
binding		9 strips 2¼" x 42"
White	8½	16 A, 32 C, 96 D, 384 E, 768 F, 64 G
Backing	8¼	3 panels 31½" x 93"

*Yardage based on 42"-wide fabric.

TREE BLOCK

1. Make 768 red and white half-square units from the F patches. See page 34 for construction options.

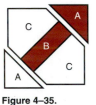

2. Construct the trunk unit with red patches A and B and white patches A and C (Figure 4–35).

Figure 4–35.
Trunk unit assembly.

3. To assemble the tree branches, sew the half-square units and the D and E patches in rows and then in sections as shown in Figure 4–36a. Sew the sections together to complete the block. Make 16 blocks.

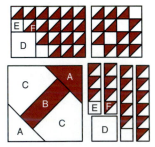

Figure 4–36.
(a) Sew squares in sections.

(b) Sew sections together to complete the block.

CHAIN BLOCK

4. Sew a red 2" strip and a white 2" strip together as shown in Figure 4–37. Cut the sewn strips in 2" sections. Use the sections to make 96 four-patches.

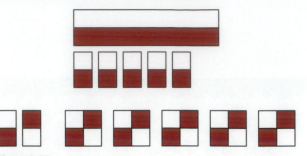

Figure 4–37.
Make 96 four-patches from strips.

5. To assemble the nine whole blocks, combine the four-patches with the D and G patches as shown (Figure 4–38).

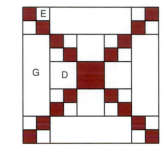

Figure 4–38.
Chain block assembly.

HALF AND QUARTER BLOCKS

7. Assemble 12 half-blocks and four quarter-blocks as shown in Figure 4–39 and 4–40.

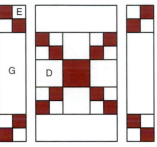

Figure 4–39.
Quarter-block assembly.

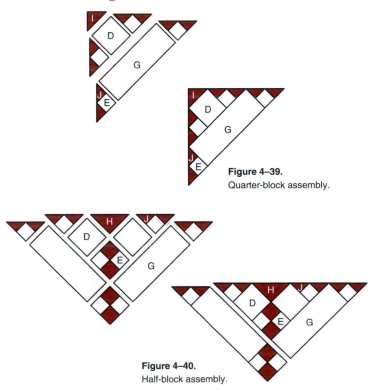

Figure 4–40.
Half-block assembly.

QUILT ASSEMBLY

8. Set blocks together, alternating tree blocks and chain blocks in diagonal (Figure 4–41).

9. For the border, sew the 2½" red strips together, end to end with diagonal seams, as needed. Cut four lengths approximately 91" from the sewn strips. Sew the border strips to the quilt and miter the corners (page 38).

10. Layer the quilt top, batting, and backing and baste the three layers together. Quilt as desired. A commercial feathered oval was quilted in background patches C/Cr and G. In the Chain blocks, the red squares have arcs on all four sides. A cross-hatched grid was used in the lower portion of the tree, and a feathered arch was quilted on both sides of the tree tops. All other areas were quilted in through the diagonal seams of the half-square units. Follow the general directions to bind the raw edges (pages 38–40).

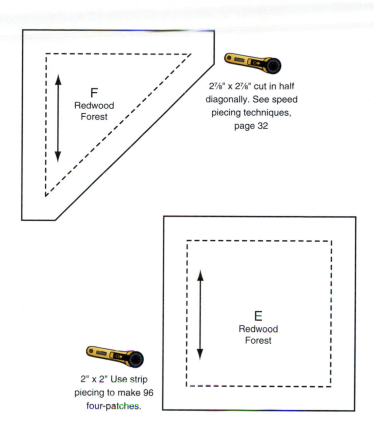

F
Redwood
Forest

2⅞" x 2⅞" cut in half diagonally. See speed piecing techniques, page 32

E
Redwood
Forest

2" x 2" Use strip piecing to make 96 four-patches.

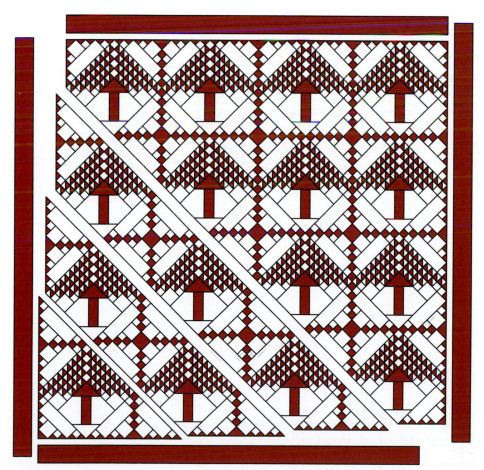

Figure 4–41.
Quilt assembly.

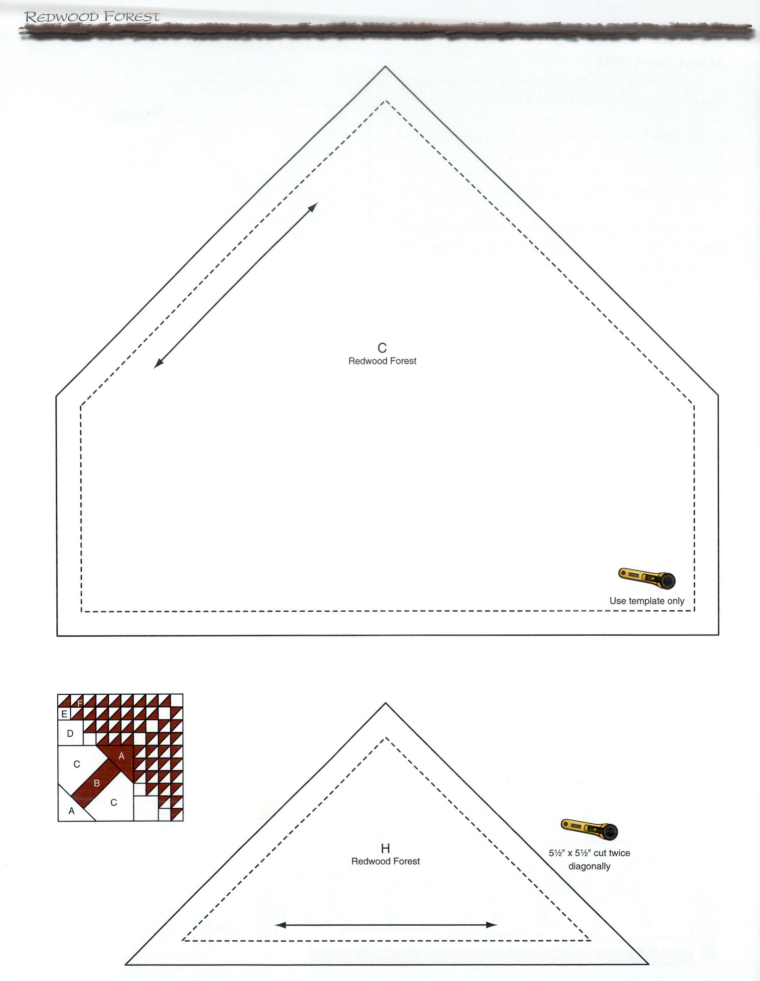

C
Redwood Forest

Use template only

E
F
D
C
A
B
C
A

H
Redwood Forest

5½" x 5½" cut twice
diagonally

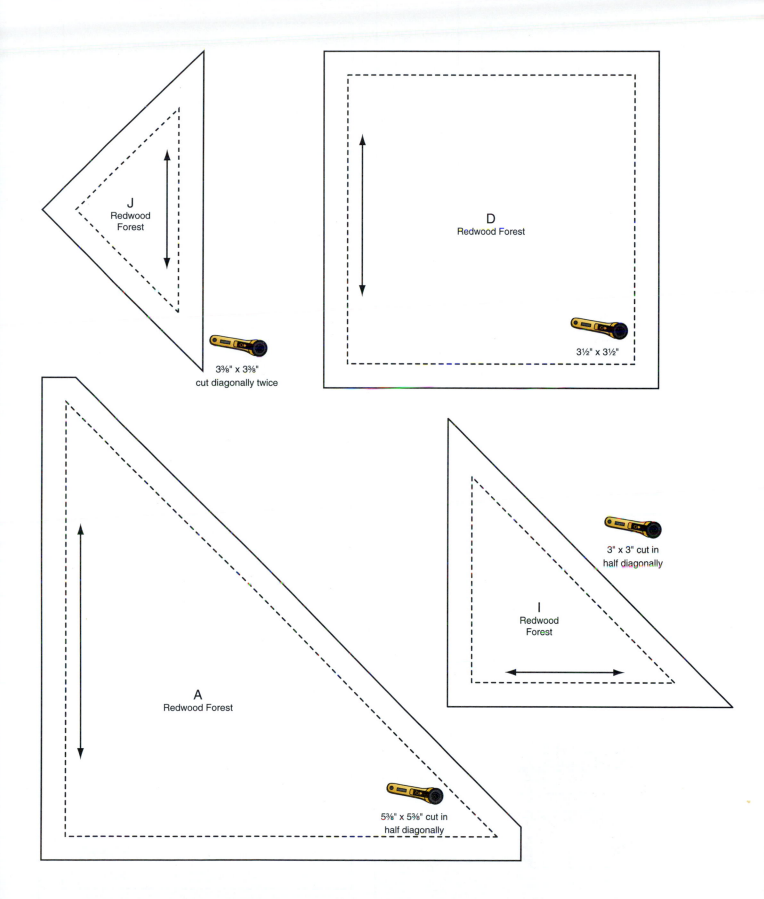

J
Redwood
Forest

3⅜" x 3⅜"
cut diagonally twice

D
Redwood Forest

3½" x 3½"

I
Redwood
Forest

3" x 3" cut in
half diagonally

A
Redwood Forest

5⅜" x 5⅜" cut in
half diagonally

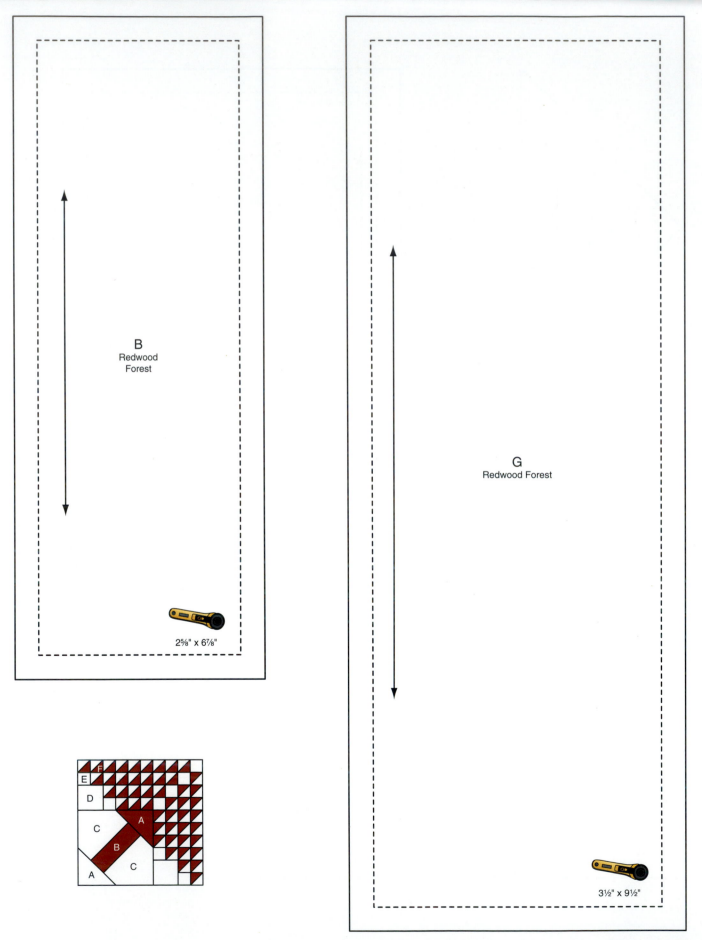

B
Redwood
Forest

2⅝" x 6⅞"

G
Redwood Forest

3½" x 9½"

PINE TREE CHRISTMAS ORNAMENT

Fabric Requirements and Cutting

Fabric*	Yards	Pieces
Tree	scraps	1 A, 1 C, 14 D
Background	scraps	2 B, 14 D, 2 E
Backing	scrap	3½" x 3½"
Batting		2½" x 2½"

*Yardage based on 42"-wide fabric.

PINE TREE Ornament (2½" x 2½") by the author.

This little ornament resembles the REDWOOD FOREST block. You can make a forest of little trees to use as holiday decorations.

Working with miniature blocks requires special techniques. All seam allowances should be pressed open rather than to one side. Trim the seam allowances to approximately ⅛" after sewing.

ORNAMENT ASSEMBLY

1. Make the half-square units for the tree branches by cutting individual red and white D triangles and sewing them together.

If you prefer, you can place a white and a red 1⅜" square right sides together. Draw a diagonal line on the top patch, corner to corner. Sew ¼" from the line on both sides. Cut on the drawn line to make two half-square units (Figure 4–42).

Make 14 half-square units.

Figure 4–42.
Sew ¼" from the drawn line. Cut on the line.

2. Join the half-square units in sections (Figure 4–43).

3. Sew the B triangles to the trunk (A patch). If you rotary cut the trunk, use a square rotary ruler to trim it even with the B patches. Add the red C patch to complete the trunk unit (Figure 4–44).

Figure 4–43.
Join units in sections.

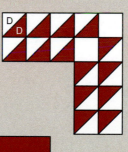

Figure 4–44.
(a) Sew two B triangles to trunk patch A.
(b) Use a square ruler to trim trunk.
(c) Sew C to trunk unit.

4. Sew the branch sections and trunk unit together to complete the block.

5. Split the batting square by pulling gently to separate it into two 2½" squares.

6. Layer the backing, batting, and pine tree. Quilt if desired.

7. Bring the backing to the front, fold the raw edge under, and appliqué the fold to the front to form a mock binding.

8. Quilt through all the layers next to "binding."

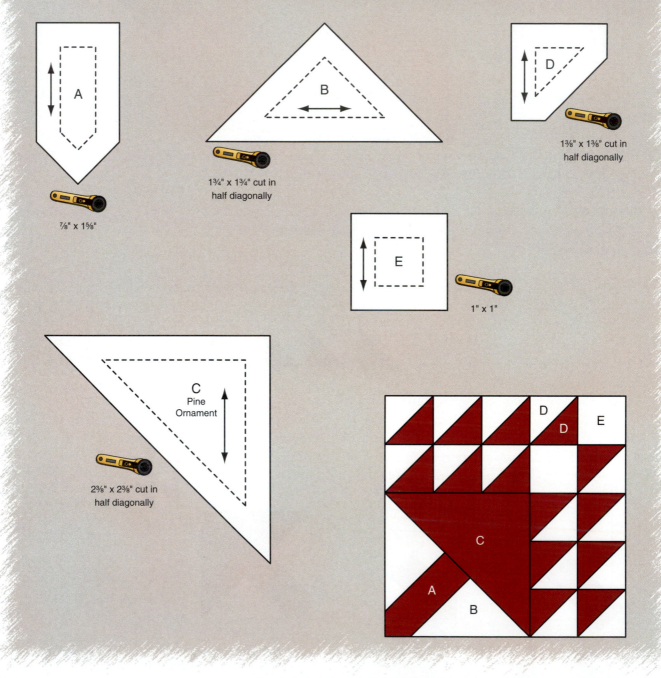

A

⅞" x 1⅝"

B

1¾" x 1¾" cut in
half diagonally

D

1⅜" x 1⅜" cut in
half diagonally

E

1" x 1"

C
Pine
Ornament

2⅜" x 2⅜" cut in
half diagonally

Territorial Trees

TERRITORIAL TREES (50" x 50") by Diane Pitchford.
An antique Pine Tree quilt with redwork inspired Diane to create this wonderful version.
She modified a quilting stencil for her embroidery design (see Resources, page 124). For best results,
mark sashing strips, cornerstones, and setting triangles on yardage, allowing extra space between each piece.
Embroider the designs before cutting the yardage to allow for drawing up during the embroidery process.

FABRIC REQUIREMENTS

Fabrics*	Yards	Pieces
Green: branches	scraps	312 B
Red:	7/8	
fruit		12 A, 48 B
border 1		5 strips 1" x 42"
binding		6 strips 2¼" x 42"
Brown: trunks	scraps	12 D, 12 F, 24 G
Cream: block	5/8	
background		24 C, 12 E, 12 Er, 12 H
Cream-print:	5/8	
branches		24 A, 288 B
Tan:	2¼	
sashes		32 strips 2½" x 8½"
cornerstones		21 squares 2½" x 2½"
side triangles		1 square 15½" x 15½"
corner triangles		2 squares 16½" x 16½"
border 2		4 strips 2½" x 53"
Backing	3¼	2 panels 28" x 54"
Batting	—	54" x 54"

*Yardage based on 42"-wide fabric.

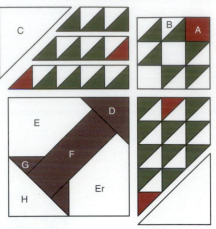

Figure 4–45.
Block assembly.

QUILT ASSEMBLY

4. Sew the blocks, sashes, and cornerstones in diagonal rows. Sew the rows together. Add the borders, mitering the corners (Figure 4–46).

5. Layer the quilt top, batting, and backing. Baste the layers together. Quilt as desired. All the cream, cream-print, and tan pieces were stipple quilted, including the embroidered areas. The stippling did not cross the embroidery, however. The tree trunks and outer border were quilted in a diagonal cross-hatch pattern.

6. Follow the general instructions on pages 38–40 to apply binding and add a label.

TREE BLOCK

1. Construct 264 green and cream-print half-square triangle units (B patches). Make 24 half-square units in red and cream.

2. Use the D, E, Er, F, G, and H patches to construct 12 trunk units (Figure 4–45).

3. Sew the half-square units and B triangles together in sections as shown. Sew the branch sections, trunk units, and C patches together to complete the blocks.

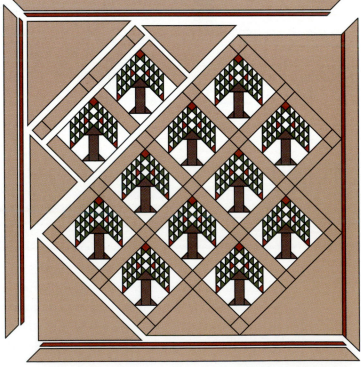

Figure 4–46.
Quilt assembly.

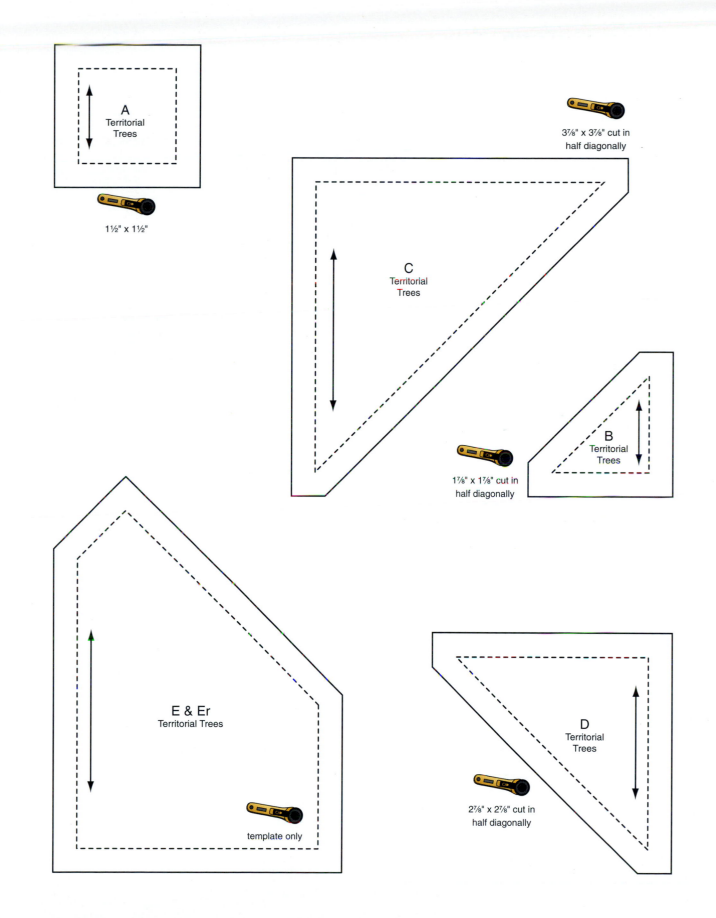

A
Territorial
Trees

1½" x 1½"

3⅞" x 3⅞" cut in
half diagonally

C
Territorial
Trees

B
Territorial
Trees

1⅞" x 1⅞" cut in
half diagonally

E & Er
Territorial Trees

template only

D
Territorial
Trees

2⅞" x 2⅞" cut in
half diagonally

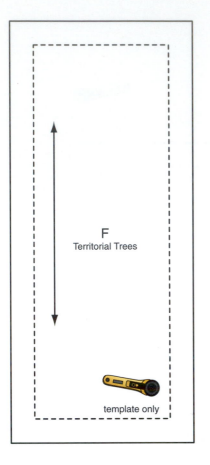

F
Territorial Trees

template only

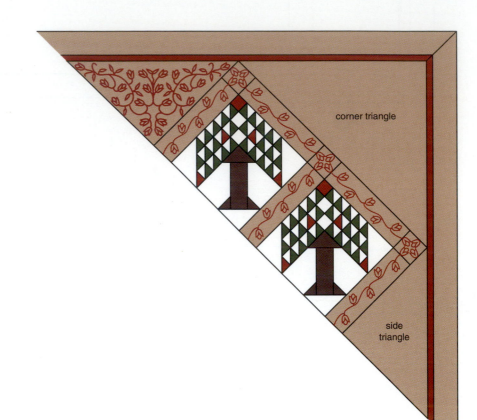

corner triangle

side triangle

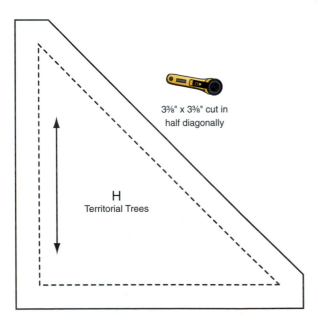

3⅜" x 3⅜" cut in
half diagonally

H
Territorial Trees

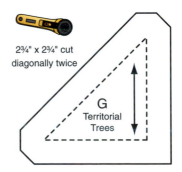

2¾" x 2¾" cut
diagonally twice

G
Territorial
Trees

Embroidery pattern for TERRITORIAL TREES sashing.

Diane Pitchford adapted this embroidery design from two commercial stencils, one by Quilting Creations International and another by StenSource International. (see Resources, page 124).

Round Robin Quilt

ROUND ROBIN QUILT (33½" x 42½") by Lois Arnold, Linda Yantis, Sue Williams, and Judi Peterson.
Just for fun, four of us made a round robin, with each person creating a block and passing it to the other three friends to add borders. The participants were asked to use a spring theme. You can make this quilt as shown, using any 3" block where the swans are, or you can use the 14" Pine Tree block as a great start to your own round-robin quilt.

Fabric Requirements and Cutting

Fabrics*	Yards	Patches
Blue 1:	1½	
block background		1 C, 1 Cr, 2 E,
		18 F, 3 G
setting triangles		2 squares 11½" x 11½"
border 2		2 strips 4⅞" x 30½"
		2 strips 4⅞" x 30¾"
sawtooth border		92 K
Blue 2:	¼	
pond section		20 H, 1 I
Green 1:	scraps	
branches		1 D, 24 F
ground under pine		1 A
sawtooth border		92 K, 4 L
vine leaves		
blossom leaves		
Green 2:		
pond section	⅓	4 I, 2 J
border 1	⅛	4 strips 1" x 17"
Green 3:	1	
vine		1 rectangle 18" x 22"
binding		5 strips 2¼" x 42"
Brown:	scraps	
trunk		1 B
pine cones		
White:	⅛	—
bunchberry blossom		
Gold:	scraps	—
blossom center		
Backing	1⅜	1 panel 37" x 46"
Batting	—	37" x 46"

1 skein green embroidery floss to match leaves
1 skein dark green embroidery floss for pine needles
Crystal seed beads (optional)

*Yardage based on 42"-wide fabric.

Round 1

The author started this round-robin quilt with a single on-point Pine Tree block in the center, but you can start with several blocks set side by side or on point. You can frame the blocks or add sashing. There are no rules for beginning a round robin.

Pine Tree block

1. Sew a blue and a green F triangle together to make a half-square unit. Make 18 half-square units for the branches.

2. Assemble the trunk unit by following Figure 4–47. Y-seam stitching is necessary in this unit. Sew C and Cr to trunk B, leaving a ¼" seam allowance at the base of the trunk unsewn. Sew A to B, stitching from edge to edge. Match the edges of C and A and sew from the outside edge, stopping at the seam line. Backstitch to lock threads. Repeat for patch Cr.

3. Sew the half-square units, remaining green F triangles, and E triangles into sections, as shown in Figure 4–48. Sew the sections together to complete the block.

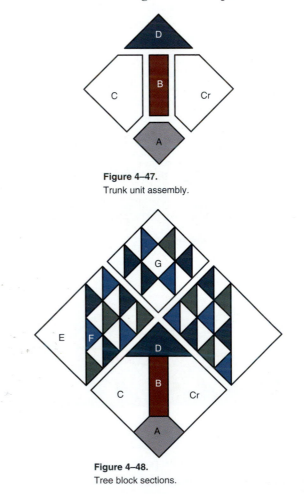

Figure 4–47.
Trunk unit assembly.

Figure 4–48.
Tree block sections.

ROUND 2

Linda Yantis added a narrow green border and setting triangles to put the tree block on point. She then embroidered pine needles and appliquéd pine cones to the upper-left triangle. To the lower-right triangle, she appliquéd and embroidered a bunchberry blossom, bud, and leaves.

Narrow border and setting triangles

1. Sew one 1" x 17" green border strip to each side of the tree block and miter the corners, following the instructions on page 38.

2. Cut the blue 11½" squares in half diagonally to make four setting triangles. Attach one triangle to each of the four sides of the bordered tree block to set the block on point.

Pine cones

3. Using a window or light box for backlighting, trace the pine needles on the upper-left setting triangle. Embroider the pine needles behind the pine cones with a stem stitch and green embroidery floss.

4. Transfer the pine-cone pattern to template plastic or freezer paper and cut the template on the line. Draw around the template on the right side of a brown scrap. Cut three pine cones, adding ⅛"–¼" seam allowances by eye as you cut. Appliqué the pine cones on top of the embroidered pine needles. Finish by embroidering the pine needles that cross in front of the pine cones.

Bunchberry blossom

5. Make templates for pattern pieces 1, 2, 3, 5, and the three-dimensional bud circle (piece 4). Trace the lines indicating leaf separations and veins on the leaf template.

6. Draw around the templates on the right side of the appropriate fabrics. Transfer the leaf separations and veins to the leaf fabric, but don't cut the leaf shape yet. Cut the other fabric pieces, leaving a ⅛" to ¼" seam allowance.

7. Appliqué the blossom to the leaf shape, and appliqué the gold center to the blossom. Embroider the leaf separations and veins, then cut the leaf shape,

leaving an allowance as before. Appliqué the leaf shape in place on the lower-right setting triangle.

8. For the bud, fold the 1¼" circle in half and then in thirds, overlapping them slightly. Tack the base of the folded circle in place on the leaf shape. The tip of the bud should remain loose. Appliqué piece 5 over the folded bud. Embroider around the edge of piece 5. If desired, embellish the flower and leaves with seed beads and French knots after the quilting has been completed.

ROUND 3

Judi Peterson added swans in a pond, using a design by Toni Smith (see Resources, page 124). In the journal that accompanied the quilt on its rounds, Judi wrote, "Near my home in the state of Washington, there were always swans in the lake at the edge of the pine tree forest."

Pond section

1. Make five 3" blocks from your favorite pattern. The blocks can be traditionally or paper-foundation pieced.

2. Add the H setting triangles to the sides of the blocks. Add the I triangles, as shown in Figure 4–49.

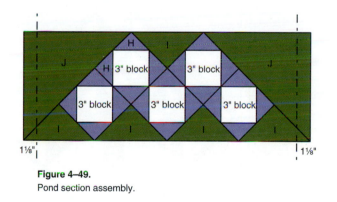

Figure 4–49.
Pond section assembly.

3. Sew the blocks and I triangles in diagonal rows, then sew the rows together. Add the J triangles.

4. Trim approximately 1⅛" from both sides of this section. It should measure 21¾" x 9½", including seam allowances.

3. Sew the pond section to the bottom edge of the tree section.

ROUND 4

Sue Williams added a plain border and a sawtooth border containing 92 half-square units and four plain green corner squares. The plain border was appliquéd after it was sewn to the quilt.

Borders

1. Sew 4⅞" x 30¾" blue borders to sides of quilt. Sew 4⅞" x 30½" blue borders to top and bottom of quilt (Figure 4–50).

2. From the green and blue K triangles in the sawtooth border, construct 92 half-square-triangle units that finish 1½" square.

3. Referring to Figure 4–50, sew 20 half-square triangle units together to form the top border and 20 for the bottom border, reversing the sawtooth design at the center. Sew 26 half-square triangle units together to form each side border, reversing at the center.

4. Sew one row of 20 half-square triangles to the top and one to the bottom of the quilt. Sew one green L square to each end of the side borders and sew the borders to the quilt.

VINE AND LEAVES

When the author received the quilt back from her three friends, she decided that the plain border would provide a wonderful backdrop for an appliquéd vine with leaves.

1. For the vine, cut eight strips ¾" in width, on a 45° angle, from the green 18" x 22" rectangle (Figure 4–51). Sew the eight strips together to form one bias strip at least 175" long.

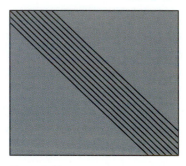

Figure 4–51.
Cutting ¾" strips from the green rectangle.

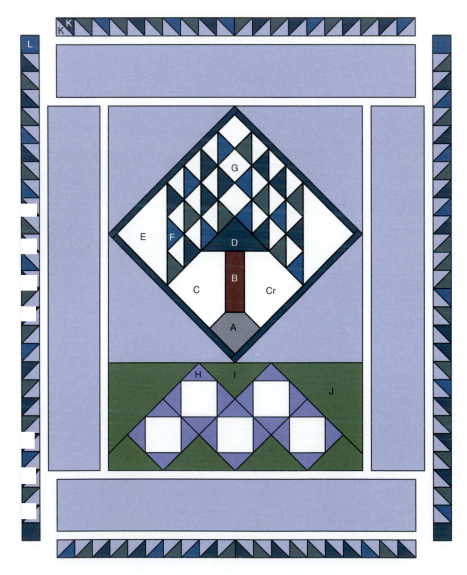

Figure 4–50.
Quilt assembly.

2. With a chalk pencil, mark a line ¼" from one edge along the length of the bias strip. Press under a ¼" allowance on one short end of the bias strip.

3. With wrong sides together, fold the opposite long edge to meet the chalk line and press in place (Figure 4–52).

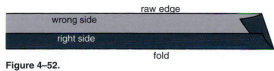

Figure 4–52.
Fold edge of bias strip to meet chalk line.

4. Make templates from the vine-repeat pattern and the corner pattern. Press the border strips in half in both directions. Use the pressed folds as guidelines for placing the vine. Starting in the middle of each border strip, use the templates and a pencil to lightly draw the vine pattern on the border. Extend the lines in the repeat pattern as needed to connect with the corner pattern.

5. Align the raw edge of the bias strip with the drawn line on the border. Pin the vine in place all the way around, overlapping the ends by at least ¼". Cut off the excess, following the diagonal of the beginning edge. Tuck the trimmed end into the folded end.

6. Using either the sewing machine or a very small hand stitch, sew along the chalk line on the bias strip all the way around to attach the first side of the vine. Trim the raw edge to ⅛" beyond the stitching.

7. Bring the folded edge of the bias strip over to meet the drawn guideline on the border. With invisible appliqué, stitch the second side of the vine in place. Appliqué the joining edge to secure the ends.

8. Make a plastic template from the leaf shape given. Trace around the leaf template on the right side of a variety of green fabrics to make 114 leaves. Cut around each leaf shape, leaving a ⅛"–¼" turn-under allowance. Pin the leaves along both sides of the vine in a pleasing arrangement. Use needle-turn appliqué to secure the leaves in place.

FINISHING THE QUILT

Layer the backing batting and quilt top. Pin- or thread-baste to secure the layers. Quilt as desired. For the quilt in the photo, the pine needles, bunchberry, vine, and leaves were outline quilted. The green border was quilted in the ditch, and all the blue areas were free-hand quilted in a meandering open stipple. The trunk is meander quilted to resemble bark. Bind the quilt's raw edges, following instructions on pages 38–40.

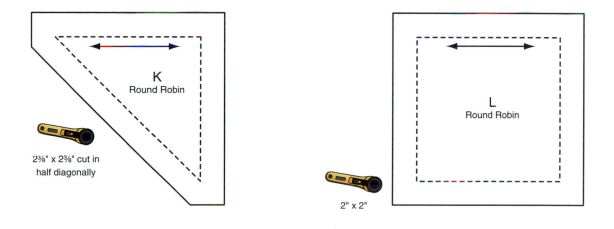

K
Round Robin

2⅜" x 2⅜" cut in
half diagonally

L
Round Robin

2" x 2"

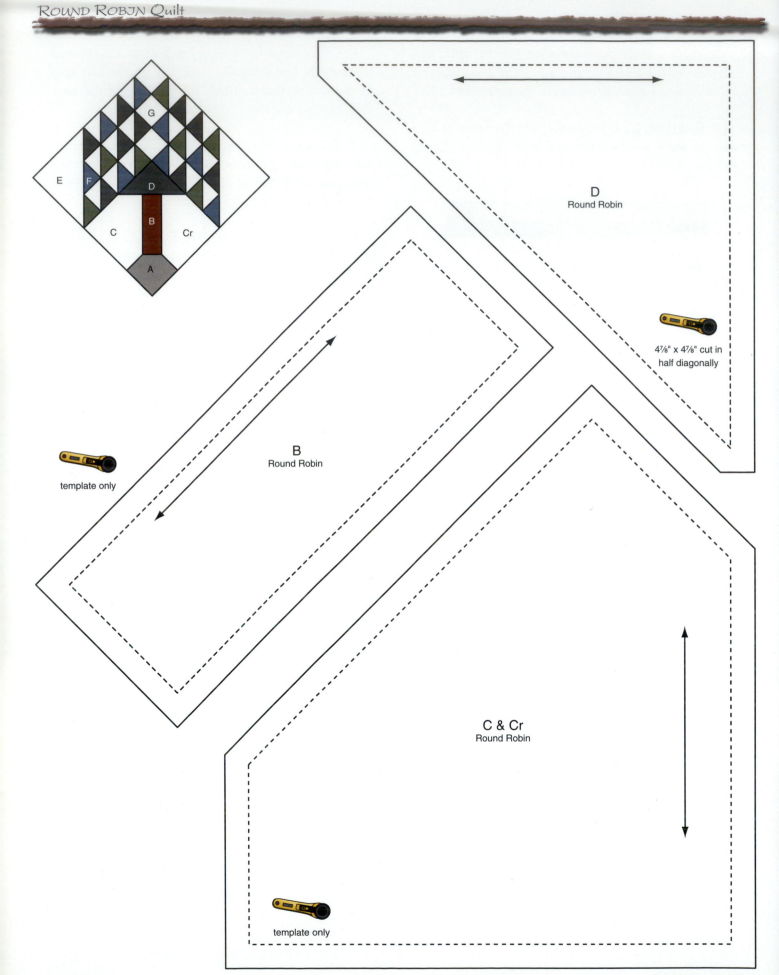

D
Round Robin

4⅞" x 4⅞" cut in
half diagonally

B
Round Robin

template only

C & Cr
Round Robin

template only

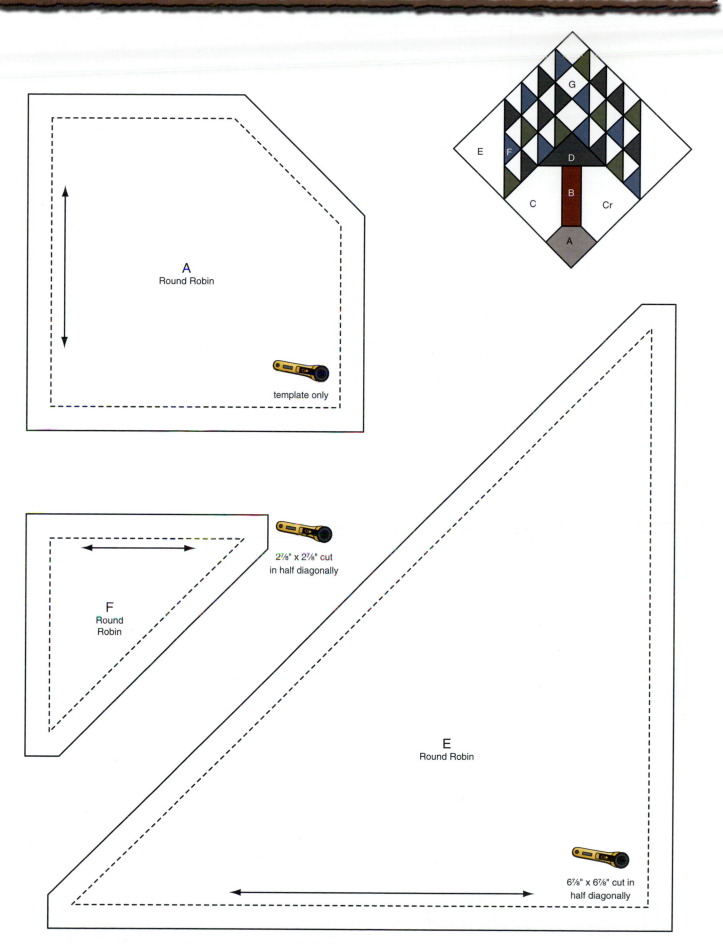

A
Round Robin

template only

F
Round
Robin

2⅞" x 2⅞" cut
in half diagonally

E
Round Robin

6⅞" x 6⅞" cut in
half diagonally

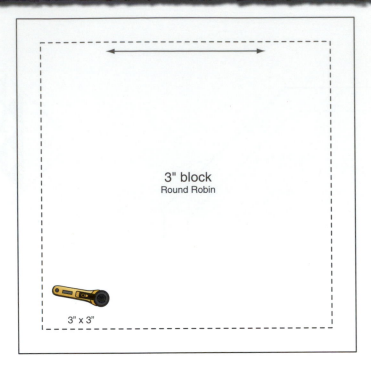

3" block
Round Robin

3" x 3"

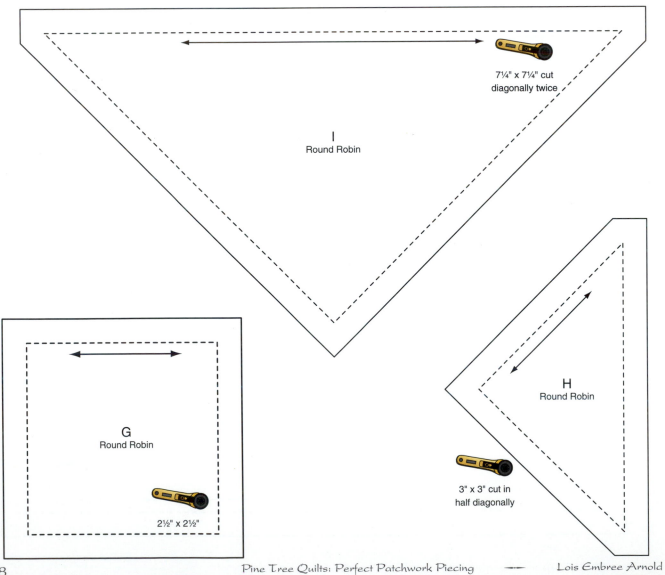

7¼" x 7¼" cut
diagonally twice

I
Round Robin

H
Round Robin

3" x 3" cut in
half diagonally

G
Round Robin

2½" x 2½"

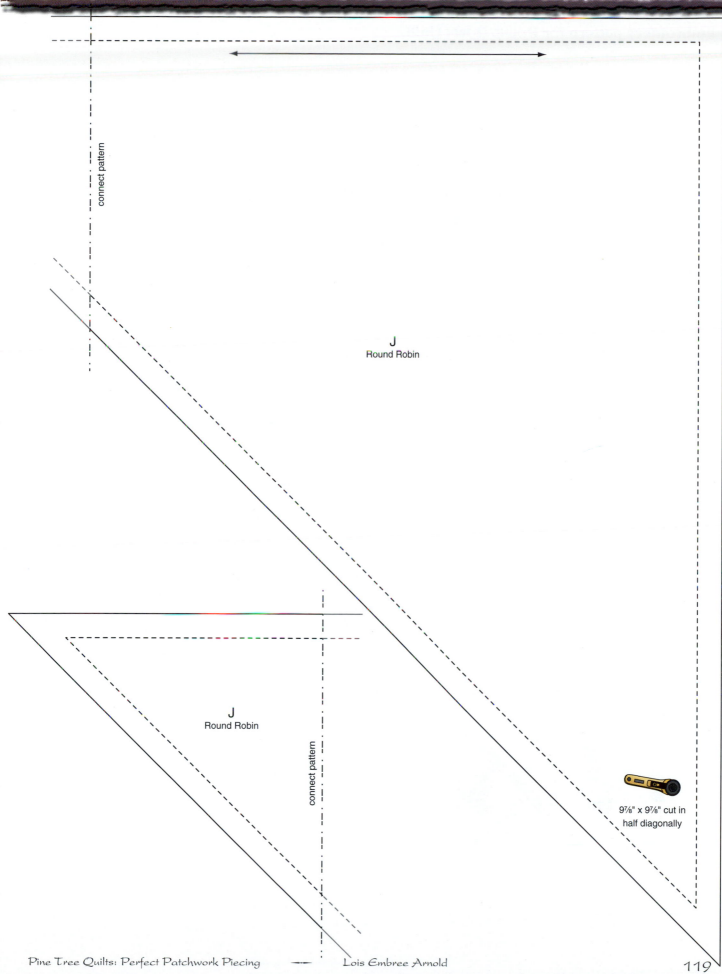

connect pattern

J
Round Robin

J
Round Robin

connect pattern

9⅞" x 9⅞" cut in
half diagonally

Embroidery pattern for ROUND ROBIN Quilt.

Linda Yantis © 1999

Detail of ROUND ROBIN Quilt.

Embroidery pattern for ROUND ROBIN Quilt.

4

5

3

2

1

Linda Yantis © 1999

leaf

flower bud

Detail of ROUND ROBIN Quilt.

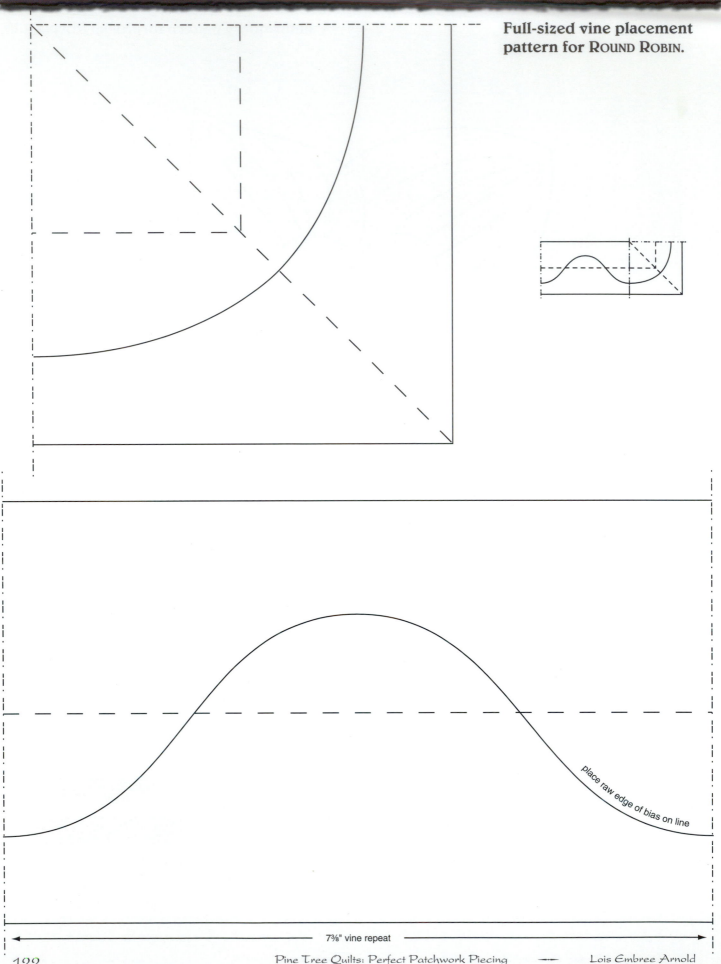

Full-sized vine placement pattern for Round Robin.

place raw edge of bias on line

7⅜" vine repeat

Bibliography

Atkins, Jaqueline M., and Phyllis A. Tepper, *New York Beauties, Quilts from the Empire State*, Dutton Studio Books, NY, in association with the Museum of American Folk Art, NY, 1992.

Beyer, Jinny, *Patchwork Patterns*, EPM Publications, Inc., McLean, VA, 1979.

Brackman, Barbara, *Clues in the Calico*, EPM Publications, Inc., NY, 1989.

Browning, Bonnie K., *Borders & Finishing Touches*, American Quilter's Society, Paducah, KY, 1998.

Cargo, Robert T., "Long Remembered an Alabama Pioneer and Her Quilts," *Quilt Digest #3*, Quilt Digest Press, San Francisco, CA, 1985.

Cochran, Rachel, Rita Erickson, Natalie Hart, Barbara Schaefer, *New Jersey Quilts*, American Quilter's Society, Paducah, KY, 1992.

Finley, Ruth, *Old Patchwork Quilts and the Women Who Made Them*, J.B. Lippincott Co., Philadelphia, PA, 1929.

Hinson, Dolores, *Quilting Manual*, Hearthside Press, Inc., NY, 1966, 1970.

Ickes, Marguerite, *The Standard Book of Quiltmaking and Collecting*, Dover Publications, Inc., NY 1959.

Laury, Jean Ray and the California Quilt Project, *Ho For California*, EP Dutton, NY 1990.

Marston, Gwen, and Joe Cunningham, *Mary Schaefer and Her Quilts*, Michigan State University Museum, East Lansing, MI, 1990.

Martin, Nancy J., *Threads of Time*, That Patchwork Place, Bothell, WA, 1990.

Oklahoma Quilt Heritage Project, *Oklahoma Heritage Quilts*, American Quilter's Society, Paducah, KY, 1990.

Sienkiewicz, Elly, *Papercuts and Plenty*, C&T Publishing, Lafayette, CA, 94549.

Young, Helen Frost, and Pam Knight Stephenson, *Arizona Quilt Project*, Grand Endeavors, Northland Publishing, Flagstaff, AZ, 1992.

Resources

Toni's Treasures
480 N. 3rd W.
Rigby, ID 83442
(800) 397-1684
www.srv.net/~tonistre/tonis.html
Paper-pieced Swan pattern

Quilters' Ranch, Inc.
P.O. Box 7646
Chandler, AZ 85246-7646
(602) 940-9682 Fax (602) 940-9408
www.trianglesonaroll.com
Triangles on a Roll

Martingale Company
That Patchwork Place
P.O. Box 118
Bothell, WA 98091-0118
(800) 426-3126
http://www.patchwork.com
Bias Square® Ruler

Omnigrid® Inc.
1560 Port Dr.,
P.O. Box 663
Burlington, WA 98233
(800) 755-3530 Fax (360) 757-4748
http://www.omnigrid.com
Omnigrid Rulers

Olfa® Products Group
Division of World Kitchen, Inc.
P.O. Box 747
Plattsburgh, NY 12901-0747
(800) 962-6532 Fax (514) 342-9760
Olfa Mat and Olfa Rotary Cutter

Quilting Creations International
P.O. Box 512
Zoar, OH 44697
(330) 874-4741
Quilting stencils

StenSource International, Inc.
18971 Hess Ave.
Sonora, CA 95370-9724
(209) 536-1148
www.stensource.com
Quilting stencils

About the Author

As a third generation quiltmaker, Lois Arnold has lived with quilts all her life. Being a "country girl" at heart, Lois loves to be surrounded by antiques and traditional quilts, but she makes both traditional and innovative quilts. She enjoys using a variety of techniques and sets up challenges for herself on each project. Her passion for the pursuit of perfection in patchwork has earned her the title of "Princess of Precision" among her quiltmaking friends.

Lois began teaching quiltmaking in 1980 when friends asked her to teach them to quilt. Since that first class, she has taught in a variety of shops and class settings. Her greatest thrill is to see what she calls "the great aha" as students catch on.

Desiring to know more about quilts and to know other quilters, Lois attended the Land of Lincoln Quilt Symposium in 1982. She went back home determined to find local quilters. Later that year, Lois became the founding president of a guild that grew from five to one hundred members in two years.

Her quilts, wall quilts, and quilted clothing have been exhibited in galleries and quilt shows from coast to coast. Lois has won awards in local, regional, and national shows. Her quilts have appeared in books and magazines, and she has been a guest on the "Simply Quilts" television series.

Lois resides in Chandler, Arizona, with her husband, Gary. In addition to quilting, she enjoys reading mysteries, entertaining, looking for great antiques, and trying to keep flowers alive in the desert sun.

OTHER AQS BOOKS

This is only a small selection of the books available from the American Quilter's Society. AQS books are known worldwide for timely topics, clear writing, beautiful color photos, and accurate illustrations and patterns. The following books are available from your local bookseller, quilt shop, or public library.

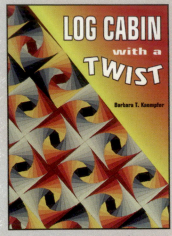

#4545   us$18.95

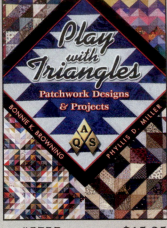

#5737   us$15.95

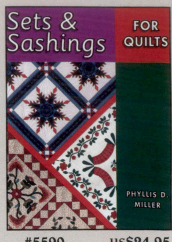

#5590   us$24.95

#5761   us$22.95

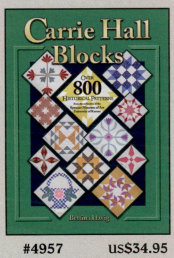

#4957   us$34.95

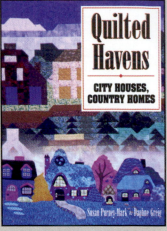

#5336   us$22.95

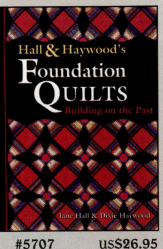

#5707   us$26.95

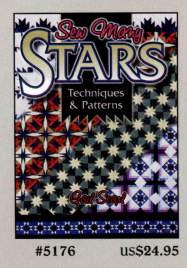

#5176   us$24.95

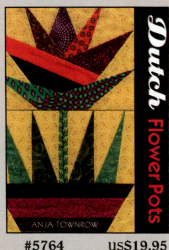

#5764   us$19.95

Look for these books nationally or call 1-800-626-5420